Pleas

MIND
ON
A CASE OF SUCCESSFUL
ADDICTION RECOVERY
FIRE

MIND
ON
FIRE

A CASE OF SUCCESSFUL
ADDICTION RECOVERY

PHILIP MULS

For information about this title or to order other books and/or electronic media, contact the publisher:

Philip Muls
www.facebook.com/philmuls

ISBNs
Print: 9789082820713
eBook: 9789082820706

Printed in the United States of America

Cover and Interior design: 1106 Design

TABLE OF CONTENTS

CHAPTER 1

INTRODUCTION

I am Dr. Catherine Lavorter, Head of Psychiatry at the Sankt-Alexius Clinic on the banks of Lake Geneva, Switzerland.

Here, we treat patients with severe addiction and impulse-control issues. Under my guidance, our facility and staff have gained a reputation for saving so-called "hopeless cases" from lifelong institutionalization.

I know all of this sounds very cold and clinical.

In reality, we deal with people, and I consider myself an expert when it comes to helping my patients get to a better place, by treating them on the level of mind and body and also on the level of their deeper self, their essential life force, also called "soul" or "spirit."

Our clinic is situated against the backdrop of the Swiss Alps, so in a way you could say we are modern-day

Sherpas, serving as guides at the extreme altitudes on the expedition to sobriety. We prepare the route, we make sure the ropes are in place and in general assure a safe ascent to the summit.

From my office, overlooking the shores of the crescent-shaped Lake Geneva, with its vista of exquisitely arranged vineyards, I wrote this book based on the recovery therapy conducted with my patient Peter Baer, whom I consider to be an extraordinary man.

When Peter first contacted me, he had just completed his fourth attempt to deal with his severe alcohol addiction. He had gone, yet again, through extreme withdrawal in detox and—to the outside world—seemed to have come out a sober man at the other end of twelve long weeks.

Yet, he was exceedingly doubtful about his ability to stay sober and ever lead a normal life without drinking. Rarely have I seen such a conflicting combination in a long-time addict of both fear and determination to remain sober. Peter would, in his own words, rather die trying than go back to hell. This book is about what happened next.

It is fair to say that Peter was a man on a mission and that his demons were unleashed during therapy before he could finally let them go. Recovery for him was like navigating a minefield of existential fears and old beliefs, each of which could explode at any time and shatter his susceptible sense of self.

Peter and his family agreed to contribute to this book with their unique perspectives on his recovery.

Peter's personal input consists of a number of stories I encouraged him to write during his frequent business trips in Asia. These travel vignettes are quite remarkable, as the reader will soon discover. You could say that writing them actually showed him the way back home.

The parts written by his son and daughter bring to life the realities of living with an addict with the brutal honesty of the young voice. And finally there is the silent contribution of his wife, who plays a major role in his recovery, behind the scenes.

I have been trained to take an objective, dispassionate view of the disease of addiction. This sometimes makes me seem detached and unemotional in my responses, while, as you will see, Peter is great at expressing his very personal sense of his condition and is not afraid to show his despair, at times. But he also shows great courage to turn this same despair into insights which can greatly benefit the reader.

This case has moved me to my core. Together with Peter, I discovered that melancholy has its very own beauty and is not a disorder that needs to be cured. To live a good, sober life is not to be immune to sadness.

CHAPTER 2

ROCK-BOTTOM

BY CATHERINE LAVORTER

I first met Peter in the summer of 2013. He was a forty-seven-year-old business executive who was traveling the world extensively as a director in a global software company.

His many travels took him from Beijing to Moscow and from Bangalore to Singapore. A rainmaker for his company, the incessant wheeling and dealing across the globe while being a high-functioning alcoholic had clearly taken its toll on the man.

Peter's wife, Laura, runs her own consulting business and also travels a great deal. They have two grown-up children—a son, Wolf, and a daughter, Winter. The Baers live in a lovely mansion right here on the shores of Lake Geneva.

Both Peter and Laura are accomplished profes-
sionals, yet they were unable to prevent the family unit
from running completely off track. It is safe to say that
Peter's addiction to alcohol was a key driver for their
difficulties, but definitely not the only source of trouble.

A seasoned corporate warrior, Peter came across
as sophisticated and worldly-wise, and yet unable to
cope without alcohol.

Fully identified with his mind, Peter was at the
extreme end of the spectrum of true thinkers, people
who are unaware they even exist beyond their thoughts
and who are out of touch with their emotions. And in
that very rational way of his, he was very conscious of
the problematic function that alcohol played in his
life by letting him escape from his mind.

To illustrate that his preoccupation with endless
thinking was not something recent, Peter brought to
our very first session a picture of himself as a twenty-two-
year-old, sitting on a marine dock, watching a stunning
sunset on the coast of Amalfi, Italy. I must admit that
I had never before seen a young face so troubled by
thought in such a wonderful setting, where you would
expect the exact opposite. The glorious light of dusk in
Amalfi made for an amazing picture, and yet the viewer
is drawn to the distraught expression on the boyish face,
which can be read only as a mix of despair and hope.

Peter brought the photo because, to him, it captures
his whole life in a single image. With a look of nostalgia

6

on his face, he told me the photograph had been taken on a legendary summer break in the Mediterranean together with three girls and one other boy, straight out of college, roaming through wondrous Italy. Yet there he was in that picture, sitting in isolated rumination, regretting things from the past and worrying about things to come.

At that young age, right after graduation, the world was open to him, yet he felt ambiguity about the sense of life and he considered his sharp mind to be a curse and a blessing at the same time. A mind that in the years to come, would go and create its own problematic interpretation of the world and would come to see alcohol as a necessary coping mechanism.

Early on in therapy, Peter realized that the key to his recovery was to take a step back from his own toxic thoughts, without the involvement of alcohol. He came to see that problems of the mind cannot be solved on the level of the mind. He felt he needed to go deeper, below his scattering thoughts and emotions.

When he first spoke to me on the phone, he explained that he had just been released from a detox center and was certain he would relapse in the next few hours if not helped. He sounded anxious and sincere, and because I had a cancellation in my schedule, I proposed to see him that same evening.

He entered my office at seven PM sharp, and right away, he struck me as a man in pain. He looked young for his age, with kind blue eyes, but his expression was tense, and his voice was slightly trembling, as if he had been bottling up his emotions to the point of eruption. Beyond a doubt, he needed immediate support in order to stay sober. The effect of the twelve weeks he had just spent in rehab had already worn off, it seemed.

I asked him to recall his darkest hour, a recent moment of deep suffering that had made him decide to stop drinking and get himself committed into rehab. A vivid reliving of the deep despair that hitting rock-bottom brings about can provide a strong defense against imminent relapse. I asked him to tell me about this recent nadir event in the present tense, to replay the tape in this very moment and make him re-experience the horror with the same emotional intensity and hence find his resolve.

Peter's face visibly turned ashen as he worked at making his rock-bottom moment resurface. As I would find out later, he was an excellent pupil when it came to taking instructions and doing exactly what was expected of him. No doubt this was also the reason for his professional success. His sharp intellect could rapidly find its way to any objective, like a guided missile.

"It's three AM on a Wednesday night," he said in a husky voice, looking straight at me, "now three months ago. I wake up in a cold sweat, trembling violently from severe withdrawal. My heart is beating in my throat, and I feel nauseous and dizzy. My bed linens are soaked with sweat. It's been only five hours since my last drink, but my body has woken me up from a booze-induced sleep because it needs alcohol, and it needs it now."

I was somewhat taken aback by this forceful start. When I found my bearings, I said, "You've got the right tone; try now to face the horror of the moment, and describe it to me, however painful."

"I am scared shitless because it is clear I've lost all control. The addiction has taken full possession of me. It seems I've crossed an invisible line, and alcohol is now the new boss. I have been spiraling down for a while now, like a helicopter with a broken tail fin in a lethal spin. And it seems that, tonight, it has come to a point where forces of nature will dictate what will happen next. I feel I have zero options."

"You accurately describe the overwhelming feeling of powerlessness that comes with the addictive state," I said, encouraging him to continue. "What else is going on in your mind?"

"Apart from the horrific cravings for booze, there is also the fear that I will suffer a seizure if I do not get alcohol in me fast. This has happened before, and I don't want it to happen again. My willpower seems to be unplugged from its source; my body and mind are conspiring against all better judgment."

"Losing control like that can be extremely scary. What happens next?"

"I'm sitting up straight in bed, in the spare bed-room up in the attic of our house. I feel utterly alone. By then, I've been sleeping alone for more than a year because my wife, Laura, has shut me out of the master bedroom after many reproachful discussions about my drinking. She has lost all respect for me after my recent series of lapses, and so have I. A familiar black desperation washes over me."

I could picture him up there, all alone in that dark attic room under the roof, craving a drink. I really felt for him, but it was my job not to become emotionally involved.

"What did you do then, Peter?"

"Well, Doc, they say stopping is simple. Just do not bring a drink up to your mouth. If only that was an option."

He waited for a minute and said, "So I am sitting there, thinking I do not want to go downstairs to the kitchen, yet I am certain I will. It is three AM, for God's sake; only an insane person would drink now. But my body screams for alcohol to make it through the night. The cold shivers, the trembling, the chest pains, the all-consuming nausea. All of that will go away imme-diately with the next drink. Of that I am sure."

"I understand it was anything but simple," I responded. "If it had been, we would not be sitting here now. So did you go down to the kitchen to get that drink?"

"I remember putting my bare feet down on the hardwood floor. I try to stand up but feel shaky. I shuffle around in the dark until I find the light switch. I curse myself for being weak, and I'm thinking, *This might be your last chance to save yourself—do not go down.*"

He shook his head and continued: "Yet my body responds by calling out for alcohol vehemently, and a familiar voice in my head says, *I am a victim, and this is a disease. I cannot handle this on my own; the delirium and tremors will kill me if I just stop cold turkey. I will just get that one drink to make it to the morning.*"

"All of these considerations are quite rational," I say, "despite the state you were in. This tells me you did not act on impulse. You really felt there was nothing else you could do." From his composure, I could tell that the worst was still to come.

"Yes, I go ahead and navigate the stairs all the way down, putting both feet together on each step, just as an old man would. When I'm finally down in the kitchen, I do not switch on the light. I open the fridge, and, in its divine light, I see the half-empty bottle of white wine I knew would be there. The bottle sparkles like a sliver of heaven in my hell. I make a last, futile attempt to resist, forcing myself to think the wine is poison. The voice in my head takes the cue and says, *Sure, but it is your poison, your lifeline.*"

"Heaven and hell—those capture the duality of drinking, all right," I said.

"Yes, well, I can't be bothered to locate a glass. I just raise the bottle to my lips and drink. The cold, golden liquid eases down my throat and fills my stomach. It creates a burning sensation that radiates throughout my body. A wonderful feeling of deep relief rushes to my head and takes away all the pain. I get tears in my eyes from joy and self-hate, in equal measures. Deep emotions overwhelm me."

"You must have been deeply conflicted," I said.

He nodded. "While I'm drinking, I know this is but a short truce. The more alcohol I consume now, the more brutal the withdrawal effects will be. There is no doubt in my mind that I will pay for this in the long run. A feeling of complete aloneness and mortal dread overtakes me. Deep down, I know that I am committing involuntary suicide."

"I must admit, I get shivers all over when I hear you tell your story," I said. "I can only imagine how you must have felt there in your kitchen, realizing you're caught in a lethal loop."

I let this sink in for a minute.

"However, you sound very authentic, which tells me you have come a long way in understanding the disease that is alcoholism. You're certainly not in denial. But why is it, Peter, that you needed to see me urgently today? You told me you'd just made it through rehab once again. Is that not a solid basis to abstain? Surely you do not want to go back to the horror of what you just described?"

"I had myself committed three times before," he said, "and I relapsed every time on the very first day out. This time around, I am determined to make it, but I find myself in hell."

"Describe what 'hell' means to you."

He didn't have to think about this. 'Hell' was clearly all around him.

"The bottle is so close, I can touch it. I can actually taste the booze on my lips." He looked discouraged and agitated at the same time. The words came out in quick succession. "I keep thinking, *Why would this time be different? In the final analysis, I will drink again.* The reality is that I still feel like a dry drunk, with my sobriety balancing on character effort only. White-knuckle stuff, you know, as opposed to a bottom-up recovery."

There was a short pause, and then again a cry for help.

"At this very minute, I have to tell you, I feel my inner resources depleting fast. I am afraid I will cave soon. I might go for a drink once I leave your office. Honest to God."

I tried to be calm and composed, as a counterweight to his mental turmoil. "I believe you underestimate the power in yourself to stay clean. You clearly have the will to recover. You will not drink today. You will not drink tomorrow. Think about your rock-bottom moment when you need to. That will stop you from actually reaching for the bottle."

He looked like a lost puppy.

"I will see you in two days' time. Trust yourself—you are stronger than you think." I felt I needed to send him off with a challenge. "There are no guarantees, but I feel confident that, together, we can instill a lasting sobriety. It is clear we need to dig deeper, give you a reason to want to live a sober and authentic life, and even enjoy it. But this type of personal transformation can be a long journey. Are you up for it?"

"This is my last chance, Doc. I know that if I touch alcohol again—even one small sip—all of my resolve will be gone, forever. So yes, I am up for it. But still, I fear that I will relapse before I see you again. My past shows that obviously I lack the backbone to see this through to the end. It seems I cannot cope on my own."

I kept my silence and gave him a look of encouragement.

With a faint smile, he added: "Clearly, you have more faith in me than I do."

"Peter, I need you to trust me in this. You will not drink. I will see you the day after next, and you will tell me here in this office how you did it."

When Peter left my therapy room that day, I felt a heavy responsibility descend upon me. I believed him when he said it was his last chance, but I was convinced that the tough love I had given him today was the only cure. The decision to stop drinking needed to come from him and from him alone.

There was no point in having him recommitted into rehab for yet another flying-trapeze act with a safety net. It was now or never for Peter. I had just taken away his net.

CHAPTER 3

MY DAD AND ME

BY WOLF BAER

The very last thing I expected to see this morning was my father sitting at the kitchen table when I came down to fix myself a quick breakfast before school. I'd become very used to him not being at home. I'd assumed he was still in rehab, yet there he was, in the flesh. He must have come home late last night.

He was drinking black coffee and looked up at me with a forced smile. I could tell he was nervous to be out, yet trying hard to make a stable impression for my sake. I remembered from his previous attempts at sobriety that this was when it usually collapsed, right after he got released.

My dad, a grown-up man sitting uncomfortably in his own kitchen, fighting the unbearable cravings. It scared the shit out of me.

I felt a pang of guilt that I'd not gone and visited him at the detox facility where he'd been for the last twelve weeks. These rehab places gave me the creeps.

It seemed to me that over the last two years, Dad had spent more time in treatment than at home with us. And for what? Every time he got out, he had reached for the damn bottle the very first chance he got.

Although he clearly tried to portray confidence, he looked shaky, and I was pretty sure he would go for a drink before long. I really couldn't stand to see him like this. For some reason, he reminded me of a deer, pierced by an arrow through the neck, roaming the woods until it bled to death.

Walking wounded.

That is how I saw my dad, damaged and defeated by the blows that life had dealt him. Not quite the role model I needed to deal with my own challenges.

As it happened, I was struggling with some of the same issues myself. I'd gotten myself in trouble lately due to an unhealthy mix of weed and beer in my daily routine. I wondered often whether I was genetically predisposed to be like my dad. Every time I tried to restrain myself when it came to drugs or booze, it was as if a voice inside me told me there was no point resisting, because I was just like my old man, really, an apple from the same tree, an addict in the making.

"Hey, Dad," I said as I reached for the refrigerator door.

"Hi, Son. How are you?"

"Mm, Okay, I guess. You out?"

"Yeah, they let me go yesterday evening late. I didn't want to wake you up."

I had an urge to tell him to be strong this time, but I could not. I felt it wasn't my place, given my own history with substance abuse. He saw that I was at a loss for words.

"Listen, I want you to know I am done for good. I will stay clean this time."

I winced at this. I'd heard this many times before, and yet he sounded different now. I hesitated and said, almost in a whisper.

"Sure, Dad."

"I know this is hard to believe, and I've let this family down in the past, more times than I care to remember. But I need you to give me another chance."

I felt anger well up inside of me. How many more chances did he expect us to give him?

"What is it that is going to make it different this time?

My words came out harsher than I had wanted them to. But Dad had expected something like this, and he took my accusatory question in stride.

"You have every right to be angry. I've been a bad example to you. I know you have troubles of your own, and it kills me that you do not trust me to help you. Let me prove to you I can do this."

I did not know what to think. I was not used to seeing him in such a humble state. Usually he was remorseless and domineering. Or completely indifferent.

"I can't just take you on your word again. Too much has happened."

"I can understand that, Wolf. Alcohol had me in its grip for a very long time. But now I'm back. Or at least I'm working very hard to get back."

"Remember that night last year when I drove my car off the road and ended up upside down in a ditch?"

"Yes, of course I do. The crash could very well have killed you and your friend Kevin. You kids came close to drowning in just a couple of inches of water. It's a miracle that you got out without so much as a scratch, both of you."

"Yeah, well. When you showed up before the police did, I was so relieved." I almost could not say the words. "Until I saw you had been drinking, that is. Your breath smelled of booze, and you were slurring your words. You couldn't even walk straight. It was horrible. I was shaken by the accident, but even more so, I instantly felt ashamed because Kevin could now see that my dad was a drunk." I had to look away. I could not face him. I looked out the window while I spoke. "You saved me, and I was grateful for that. But I was mortified that I was on a slippery slope, well on my way to becoming you. I too had been drinking when I had the accident."

My dad kept his silence. He had clearly not expected this. I wasn't even sure he had realized till now that he had shown up wasted at the scene of the accident. Maybe he thought all this time that I just had been happy that he came to my rescue. It's true that I never confronted him with how I felt about him showing up drunk, because I had been drinking as well.

Partners in crime, covering for each other. That felt really bad.

But then my father looked me straight in the eye and spoke with a determination that all but convinced me: "I'm done drinking, Wolf. No more, I promise."

"Sure, Dad."

CHAPTER 4

FIRST LOVE

BY CATHERINE LAVORTER

When he entered my office two days later, Peter looked strangely empowered. He was not the desperate man I had met on the first occasion. He seemed battle-fatigued but very much alive and soldiering on.

I caught myself scanning him for signs of intoxication but could find none. Unconsciously, I had been preparing myself for a likely confrontation with brutal relapse. I felt both relief and surprise that my strategy had worked.

He was sober all right. but it had clearly taken all of his power to remain so. His eyes were bloodshot, and his general look suggested it had been a short night.

He glanced at me with the bewildered smile of a shipwrecked person who had just washed ashore and could not believe his luck in meeting another human being.

"It sure is good to see you, Doc. It's been a long two days."

"Welcome back. How are you?"

"Well, a question has been burning in my mind," he said. "How the hell could you know I would take the challenge and stay clean? Quite the gamble on your part, was it not?"

I had anticipated this remark. "Not a gamble, Peter, but I do admit it was an educated guess. I felt you had proven over and over that you could handle rehab but what you needed now was to show yourself you could also bridge those dreaded first days out in the real world."

He nodded slowly, as if what I said seemed to make sense.

I continued. "You went into uncharted territory. You went further into sobriety than ever before, and that has earned you credibility on the road to recovery, mostly with yourself but also with me as your therapist."

He nodded again, so I continued. "In our first session, you said you lacked the backbone to abstain even for the next hours. Now, two days later, here you are, still sober. You did it, Peter, you and you alone!"

I decided to use an analogy. "If we were on Mount Everest right now, I'd say that over the last two days, you crossed over from Base Camp to Camp One, with bragging rights. And with me as your Sherpa to now further help you ascend further to Camp Two. It was necessary for you to spend these past days and nights alone, without my direct supervision, to acclimatize to this new height. I'm stretching the mountaineering imagery here." I smiled, but he did not immediately react. Instead, he looked deeply worried.

"Peter, the healing did not stop because you were not physically here in my office; your brain kept working and sorting through its priorities in an effort to move forward. And now you find yourself, to your own surprise, at a higher elevation."

He cleared his throat and said with a weak smile, "I like what you say, Doc. I like it a lot. You sure talk a good game. It feels indeed like I've moved beyond absolute beginner, so to say. Training wheels are off. The thought of that is scary, but it also feels good. I feel like somehow, I'm on more solid ground, or at a higher elevation, as you put it. At least as far as drinking is concerned, that is."

He paused, looking for the right words. "Truth is, even if I plow ahead and deal with the relentless cravings, still, I get these dark thoughts, and I can't help but wonder: Is this it, and is it worth it?"

"'Dark thoughts'? Can you elaborate?"

"I can't stop thinking about the futility and absurdity of it all. What's the point, really? I do not understand why I have to suffer so much. Is this really my life now? Is this all there is? Sobriety sucks."

I thought for a moment how best to respond to this typical reflex reaction of a long-time alcoholic. "I see," I said. "I think I know where you're going with this. It is quite common for recovering addicts to have existential doubts early on in their newfound sobriety. After all, you are looking for a surrogate meaning to life, something to replace the easy fix that alcohol was to you for so many years. There is a reason they call it liquid relief; it has been the instant solution to all your problems for so long. But the only thing alcohol ever did was to make things worse."

His eyes showed his anger and frustration. "I hear you, but with all due respect, these words get me nowhere at this point. My misery feels complete. Nothing I do or say seems to have any meaning. How do I dig myself out of this hole?"

"The first thing we have to do is to go back to the very beginning," I said. "It is important to understand how drinking became so deeply rooted in you, so we can reverse-engineer our way out of this maze you got yourself into. Tell me, what is your earliest memory of experiencing the effects of alcohol?"

Peter remained silent. He seemed irritated with me for not offering a quick solution to his acute problem of being faced with a complete lack of purpose.

He took a full two minutes to ponder my question. But when he finally spoke, he was his usual cooperative self. He understood very well he had to do the work; there was no easy way.

"I was seventeen when I went to summer camp in the mountain village of Sank-Moritz. Thirty years ago, and I still remember every street and every corner of that place. The lake, the snowy mountaintops. And I see the faces of my friends at summer camp like it was yesterday. We enjoyed each other's company against the amazing backdrop of the Swiss Alps, without a care in the world. It was, without doubt, one of the best summers of my life."

"Seventeen is a wonderful age, I remember."

"Well, Doc, it was during that holiday that I fell in love twice."

"It sounds like it was quite the summer, indeed. Tell me more. Who were these two young ladies who captured your heart?" I looked at him with a bemused smile and wondered where this was going.

"Ah, it was slightly more complicated than that. Let me explain."

I nodded for him to do so.

"A year before that summer, I developed a terrific crush on a lovely girl back home. Her name was Conny. A classic and sad case of unrequited love, it turned out to be. I know it sounds funny now, but this first rejection consumed all of me, back when I was sixteen. It took

27

me months to get over her, pure agony. Even now, my stomach hurts when I think of her. Lovesickness is a bitch, I can tell you."

He looked at me to check if I was mocking him, but I kept a serious face.

"Anyway, the summer after that little tragedy I was looking for anything but love, and yet it happened up there in the mountains. The girl's name was Sarah. She was delightful. Long blond hair and the kind of sweet smile that a young boy simply cannot resist." He clearly felt encouraged when he saw me smile.

"We were both quite innocent, at seventeen—imagine that. At the beginning of camp, I saw her in group orientation; she and I were at opposite sides of the briefing room. The group was loud and rowdy, and yet our eyes found each other and locked. I still remember that feeling of elation, when I saw her looking at me in that special way, in a sea full of people." He paused, cherishing the memory.

"Anyway, it took us three days of talking and walking side by side, hiking up and down the Alps, before anything else happened. We deliberately lagged behind the rest of the group and held hands until the mountain guide told us to catch up or go back. I remember him mumbling that he couldn't be expected to take responsibility for a couple of teenagers in love."

He was serious, and yet at the same time, his story had a lighter touch because of his funny way of narrating.

"In any case, Sarah's girlfriends started to tease her, while the boys whistled and told me in no unclear terms I should make a move or be considered a coward. You get the picture."

"Why did you wait so long to take it to the next step? Although holding hands is absolutely romantic."

"I honestly do not know that, Doc. I guess I was shy. When I finally kissed her, it was glorious."

He looked at me and paused, clearly to build up the tension.

"That was crush number one of that summer."

His romantic story in the Alps had captured my full attention and also my curiosity.

"Wonderful. I treasure some fond memories of my own at that innocent age. But what happened then? Did you fall in love with someone else?"

"Not someone, but rather something."

He seemed to enjoy my surprised look. I had a feeling I was being choreographed.

"On the very last day of camp, we crossed over the mountain pass from Switzerland into Italy, and we had lunch at this lovely outdoor fish restaurant, right on the banks of the Mont Blanc glacier river. When ordering for the group, our mountain guide asked who wanted to taste Suave, the local dry white wine."

It started to dawn on me where he was taking this. I did not want to interrupt him, but his elaborate window dressing of the story triggered a lot of questions in my mind.

"Before that day, I had never tasted alcohol, strange as that might seem now. I had no idea of its effect. I just said 'Yes' because the rest of the group did and because the wine was served by two dazzling Italian waitresses and poured from large cooled carafes."

He looked out the window at Lake Geneva.

"I remember sipping my glass and gazing with curiosity at the golden liquid. I tentatively sipped some more, as if I had a premonition that I was about to set in motion forces that I could not control. And then the strangest thing happened."

"What's that?" I found myself completely engrossed in his narrative. I was used to leading the dance in this office.

"The best feeling ever overwhelmed me. I can only describe it as pure joy. All my worries seemed to evaporate, and all the background noise in my mind stopped. All that was left was this otherworldly feeling of blissful calm. It felt like magic."

Now he was deadly serious.

"Bottom line, I fell deeply in love with alcohol, right there and then." He was done with the nostalgic reminiscing. Back to the problem that preoccupied his every day.

"That is what you wanted to hear, right? The original sin, the first bite of the forbidden apple. I remember thinking I had discovered the key to adult living. Finally, I could do away with all my inhibitions and boost my confidence in one clear sweep, just by raising a glass to my lips. And even look cool while doing it."

He waited for just a moment and then said with a sad expression: "And you know, ever since that first glass of Suave, I've never been able to be just a social drinker. I've used alcohol in order to ease my worries, to become calm, to be myself. Or so it seemed."

"So drinking seemed to fill a gap in your life right from the start—is that it?"

He nodded. "Yes, it seemed to satisfy a very basic need in me, like breathing or eating. I came to depend on it." Then he shook his head. "I have never understood how friends could stop after one drink or discipline themselves to lay off the stuff for a month or so. In stark contrast, I craved it every day, and then, much later, I needed it every hour. Which brings us back to that fateful night we discussed last time, when I woke up at three in the morning, shaking and trembling because I needed my fix. Hitting rock-bottom."

I sighed. "You kind of took me by surprise there, comparing young girls with white wine. However, I hear you, and I do believe there is deep relevance in the fact that you compare your discovery of the alcoholic high with the feeling of first love. To you, they are of the same epic importance, are they not?"

"Well, my infatuation with Sarah soon faded after we both returned home, as these summer flings do. My love for drinking, however, only became stronger and deeper with time. So I guess crush number two—the one with alcohol—was the real love affair of that summer. An affair that turned into quite the tragic and addictive relationship."

"I understand that drinking is looming large and preoccupies all of your thinking right now, but let us park it for just a moment. I want to go back to the girls for a minute."

He seemed annoyed. To him it was about the wine, not the girls.

"While Sarah, who reciprocated your affection, is now only a fond but distant memory, you still hurt from remembering Conny, who did not love you back. You said she was your real first love and the one that got away. Clearly, this is a painful thing for you to talk about, so it must have a lot of meaning. It was a first major disappointment in life, a devastating event. I want to explore that some more, go into that pain."

"What for?" he asked. "It has been ages since I last thought about Conny. I have her hidden away in a room full of hurt, it seems. You have to understand, over the years, she has taken on this larger-than-life place in my memory, while in reality, I never even got to know her up close. She's a ghost, an idealization. Talking about her feels awkward. Do we absolutely have to?"

I did not want to push him further at this point. But since it had met with so much resistance, there clearly was something there that we could not ignore. I decided on an alternate strategy.

"Our time for today is up so let me propose another route here. I know you are a thinker. Tell me, are you also a writer?"

"I used to write when I was younger. I remember I would totally get in the flow when writing essays for school and stuff. And I was told on more than one occasion that I could write a great love letter. But I've done nothing with it since. Why?"

"I want you to find the key to your hurt locker and write about Conny. Whatever comes up, write it down, free format. We can then discuss that in the next session. Or not. No pressure. But believe me, it is important to get this out of your system."

"How is Conny relevant to where I go from here?" he asked, still not quite buying it.

"First love is a meaningful event. The crushes number one and two at summer camp which you described were, in fact, numbers two and three. We have to trace it back to Patient Zero."

CHAPTER 5

LOVESICK

BY PETER BAER

A week after my sixteenth birthday, I am sitting in a classroom with twenty-two other boys, pretending to listen to a Latin teacher. Our minds are everywhere but here.

I for one cannot stop thinking about Conny. She is the reason for the lovesick state I have been in for weeks now. She is the epitome of perfection to the sixteen-year-old me. She has hazel eyes and a classic face of beauty. She is wearing a navy school dress accentuating her figure. For a moment, it makes me wonder whether the school has intended this effect when making girls wear a uniform. With her hair in a boy cut, she is simply irresistible.

I do not fight it, I am powerless. I recognize a higher force.

She walks with an air of carefree confidence, seemingly unaware of what she does to boys and men. With hindsight, that was a pretty naive thought on my part. I know by now that she was aware of her powers. Pretending she wasn't just made it perfect.

It started with a smile.

Dexys Midnight Runners are playing their signature song, "Come on, Eileen," as a backdrop to the epic scene that follows.

I watch Conny walking toward me along with two other girls, all wearing winter jackets, woolen mittens, and hats. She looks like an angel. She is laughing out loud because of something her friend said. Her gaze crosses mine, and it seems that her smile is now directed straight at me. She simply says, "Hi, don't you just love this song?"

That's it. That is all that happens. I am in awe.

Awe is called the eleventh emotion, beyond the basic ten known by science. Awe plays on the boundary between pleasure and fear, inspired by great beauty or mystery. It causes us to completely forget ourselves in a moment of great wonder, feeling the presence of something greater.

Yes, right on the mark. I am in awe.

And I am not equipped to deal with it. I manage to say a profound, "Hi, yes I do," back at her, and she gives me a coy glance that will stay with me forever.

A few days later, I ask her out in a burst of supreme confidence. She hesitates for a brief moment.

That moment lingers on in my eternity. It is a moment in which all is still possible, and yet you feel that it is not you but fate that will prevail.

She says, "No."

Later in life, I learned how to see rejection as a useful step in the pursuit of victory. What doesn't kill you makes you stronger and all that. But back then, it took me apart.

When it comes to drama, there's nothing quite like unrequited love. For weeks, I did not sleep or eat. It seemed to me that the meaning of life had been found and instantly lost again. If rejection hurts, rejection without a reason is a killer. It tortured me in the most intense way that she denied me that one date. To my endless frustration, guys who were not paralyzed by her loveliness did manage to go out with her. And they did it in a casual way, nothing to it.

That was a lesson in love right there. She needed a cool guy, a guy she had to fight for.

Why did I not know that? Why was this universal truth about the female longing not genetically pre-arranged in my moves? Why did all the males who preceded me let me go empty-handed into an unfair fight?

Thinking back on it so many years later, it makes me wonder.

Why was I in awe looking at her, but not when I looked at other girls who were even more beautiful? Why did her smile hold that much power over me, like I felt her sweet innocence was out of this world and I had to pursue her with everything I had? Why did I feel that something of existential importance had just slipped through my fingers?

Exquisitely painful as it was, I wouldn't want to have missed it. This first love, which did not go beyond "Hi," and yet took on legendary proportions in my memory, inspired me to look for experiences that brought me the same feeling of bewilderment and wonder.

But somehow, I never quite reached the same high-octane level in my emotional fuel and probably never will. By design it seems . . . you can be truly lovesick only once.

CHAPTER 6

ALCHEMY

BY CATHERINE LAVORTER

The day after our previous session, Peter had returned to work and had taken a flight to Singapore to meet with an important customer. Now ten days later, I couldn't help but wonder how he had coped with such a stressful journey and whether he had been able to withstand all the temptations and cravings that come with business travel.

His employer had shown exceptional patience and understanding for almost two years, supporting him through four stints of rehab. But recently they made it crystal clear that they wanted their golden boy back on the job, to attend to their burgeoning business in Asia.

That was a tall order for Peter, with abstinence not yet fully anchored down. To get back into the rat race too soon could derail him on the road to recovery. I was anxious to find out how he was doing.

When he entered my therapy room, Peter looked jet-lagged, yet strangely upbeat at the same time. Sharply dressed in business casual, he'd come straight from the airport. He seemed combative and higher on the assertiveness scale than I remembered. Once settled in, he confirmed in a matter-of-fact way that he was still sober. He gave off an aura of being in control, but I had a strong sense that this was only skin-deep.

Drinking as such did not seem foremost in his mind right now, and I did not want to trigger him on the topic unnecessarily. No doubt we would get there in due time.

He was eager to tell me about his business trip, but I wanted to loop back first to our last session before he could set the agenda for today. When he was in business mode, like he was now, he could be most convincing, but also quite domineering. No doubt, this combination was a redeeming quality in his world of high-pressure salesmanship. But in here, it was paramount that I remain in control of my own agenda.

"I am happy to see you in such high spirits," I said. "First of all, I must say, your story 'Lovesick' was so much more than I had bargained for. The way you described the feelings of awe and rejection through the eyes of the younger you was masterful. And that last line was a killer."

He smiled, and I continued. "It is so true that the emotional impact of a first crush often seems to outshine the romantic episodes that come later, in adult life. I'm sure your endearing love tragedy—if I can call it that—would strike a chord with most people, as teenage infatuation and rejection are about as universal as human experience can be."

Peter seemed happy with my praise. "Thanks, Doc. I had a feeling you would like it."

No lack of confidence there, I noted. "Tell me: Did the writing bring you a feeling of release, of liberation?"

He cleared his throat. "It took me a while to bring myself to write up what had been weighing me down about Conny. I tried hard to put myself back in my shoes when I was sixteen and replayed the scene from that vantage point. And all the while, I tried hard not to take myself too seriously." He chuckled for a minute and then said, in a more serious voice: "To my surprise, the writing made me reach well below the surface of my mind, down to my deeper impulses, you could say."

"Can you elaborate?"

"Well, I did not have to think about what to write, it was as if the words came spiraling up from my subconscious. When I finally read back what I had put on paper, it was like all new to me, like someone else had written it. Someone who had been observing me all this time, without my knowing it." He pondered for a minute. "Let me put it like this. The writing just happened, by letting a part of me take a step back and be a spectator to my thoughts and feelings."

I was intrigued by Peter's words. They reminded me of Eckhart Tolle's concept of *watching the thinker*. But I doubted that Peter was familiar with Tolle's work. I took a mental note to come back to this. Interesting.

He continued, "I know now that my first flame had a bittersweet hold over me, all this time. I had never really understood the symbolism of that first rejection, until now. It hurt so badly because what it really meant was *I only have this one life, and it is clear now that I will never spend it with her.*"

He took a moment and concluded, "Anyway, I think I am ready now to stop hoping for a better past with Conny. Does that make sense?"

"Perfect sense," I said. "Stop hoping for a better past. Accept what is and move on."

I saw that he needed another minute to mentally align with his own conclusions. He was gazing out of the window with a blank expression as if trying to convince himself of his own words. It was important for him to finally say goodbye to a precious but unhelpful fantasy that had haunted him all these years.

Privately, I was amused to see yet again how a first love, even a one-way infatuation, could cast a spell over the span of a lifetime. I've seen it in many other cases, both men and women. Near-fatal casualties of lovesickness. I could not help but smile with this universal pitfall, which makes us so very human. I felt it was time to move on, though.

"I have been thinking about what you said last time," I said, "about your struggles with the absurdity of it all, the apparent lack of meaning to life. As we did last week with your early strife with love, I would like to do the same now with this basic feeling of incongruity in you. I would like to go back to the origins of your existential fears."

Peter flinched at my words. It seemed I had his full attention.

"That's a big one," he said. "So much larger than a princess who did not want to date me thirty years ago."

It was clear that he was trying to cover up his insecurity on this topic with a display of bravado.

I kept quiet. He laughed nervously and continued, "You know, it literally takes my breath away, trying to grasp the enormity of life's groundlessness, the complete lack of certainty and security. It's exactly why I kept on drinking—to drown out these thoughts on all the dreadful things that could happen."

I still kept my silence. Better to let him work through this on his own. He let out a deep sigh as if to surrender to a higher power.

"Okay. Let me give it a try. I've never said these things out loud, so I do not know how they will come out. This may well sound over the top."

"I understand this is not a trivial matter," I said. "I think that, all along, these fundamental life concerns have been fueling the fire of your addiction. That is why we need to address them now. You have tried to cover them up, with layer upon layer of defense mechanism, one of which was the alcohol abuse, another your demanding job and relentless travel. Until it all came crashing down, and you had to get yourself hospitalized multiple times in order to survive."

I powered on. "We need to face your core pain head on. We can turn all that suffering into relevant insights, into deep knowledge about who you really are."

I wanted to use imagery to make my point. "You know of the legendary alchemists in the Middle Ages who allegedly knew how to turn base metals into gold. Well, I find that many patients consider that a useful analogy to help turn their pain into something positive."

He looked at me skeptically.

"Peter, I know this feels like a huge risk to you, but you can trust me. Please take your time to arrange your thoughts."

He took several deep breaths, and then the words came out in rapid succession.

"I am anxious about the notion that each and every one of us is really separate and alone on this Earth, which is spinning around its axis in eternal nothingness. It simply blows my mind to realize that the universe is completely indifferent to what happens to me. The idea of such brutal randomness drives me crazy. It makes me feel like I want to put a bullet in my head right now—get it over with." He sounded enraged.

"And what's up with the fact that I have unlimited freedom to make that kind of decision about my life, whether to end it or not, without any apparent external guideline or intervention? Is nobody watching out for me? Am I completely alone and unobserved?" He was straining himself to finish his troublesome list. Now he had a grim smile on his face.

"And let us not forget death as the grand apotheosis. It is a killer to know that I will eventually lose everything and everyone I care for, including myself. I want so very much to live, but what is the point if death can come at any moment?"

His tone was apologetic now. "Sorry, Doc. I did warn you, these are pretty dark thoughts." He turned away, facing the window, but not before I had seen the tears in his eyes.

"This is exactly what we're here for, to address these worries in an intrepid way." I refilled his empty glass with water. "Now, before we dig deeper, what is your earliest recollection of becoming aware of this dread of life and death?"

"Mm, let me think. I must have been five when I lost my grandmother. It was an absolute shock to come to the realization that people die. I simply could not believe it. At five, I had just been getting comfortable with being me, when this breaking news disrupted my reverie." He had a way with words. "This meant I could also lose my mother, whom I was extremely close to.

Up to that moment, it had not dawned on me that we could ever be separated."

He stood up and walked toward the window. With his back to me, he continued. "From then on, a constant fear of abandonment accompanied me everywhere I went. It was the end of innocence as I knew it. Gone was the carefree exploration of my world; everything had become dangerously fragile and impermanent. Death was everywhere I looked."

"Are you aware that every human being wakes up to this truth at some point?" I asked. "It could be that you were very sensitive as a child, but by no means is what you felt abnormal or strange. You were in full discovery of yourself and the world, and you were giving symbolic meaning to all the things that mattered to you." I paused for just a moment.

"Juxtaposed with that feeling of growth then comes all of a sudden this awareness of mortality. This very conflict makes the human condition . . . well, human." My words seemed to put him off balance.

"I always thought other people had the answers. Or they had discovered how to live without asking the questions. How . . . ?" He was at a real loss for words, so I took over.

"You are definitely not alone in this. In fact, let me read you something from one of my favorite books on this topic: The Denial of Death, by Ernest Becker. Do you know his work?"

He shook his head. I stood up to take the well-used book from my shelf and started reading out loud.

> What does it mean to be a self-conscious animal? The idea is ludicrous if it is not monstrous. It means to know that one is food for worms. This is the terror: To have emerged from nothing, to have a name, consciousness of self, deep inner feelings, an excruciating inner yearning for life and self-expression and with all this yet to die. It seems like a hoax, which is why one type of cultural man rebels openly against the idea of God. What kind of deity would create such a complex and fancy worm food?[1]

Taking another book from the shelf, I looked for the right quote, and said, "Another existential philosopher, Erich Fromm, wondered 'why most people did not become insane in the face of the existential contradiction between a symbolic self, that seems to give man infinite worth in a timeless scheme of things, and a body that decays and dies.'[2]

Peter was silent. It had taken all of his energy, after a twelve-hour flight, to unearth and confront this deep fear of death. I wondered whether I had not abused his fighting spirit here today by making him dive into the deep

---

1   Becker, Ernest. *The Denial of Death* (New York: Simon and Schuster, 1973)
2   Fromm, Erich. *The Art of Being* (Constable, 1993)

end. I brushed away my doubts because I had followed my instincts, and those were usually close to the mark.

"Are you all right? I know this is a lot to digest. This may have been the first time in your life that you addressed these issues head on."

"I'm okay," he responded. "Just a bit tired. But, what you just read did strike a chord. Can I borrow the books?"

I could see he was drained.

"Sure. Listen, I know you have another trip coming up before we see each other again. May I make a suggestion?"

"I have a feeling you are going to ask me again to write something?"

"We're getting into the swing of things here. What worked last time might work again. I believe that writing is a formidable way for you to bring what is hidden out into the open." I could see he liked the idea. "Anyway, this is what I have in mind. You said you were very close to your mother and that you were afraid of losing her as soon as you found out that people die—is that correct?"

"Yes, thinking about her brings tears to my eyes, even now. My mother passed away five years ago, this coming December."

"I am sorry to hear that. That must have been difficult for you, in the midst of your powerlessness with alcohol. I believe there may be a great deal of mourning that simply could not take place when you were still drinking. Could you imagine yourself writing about your mother?"

CHAPTER 7

CATHARSIS

BY PETER BAER

December 2008. I am up in my room on the twenty-third floor of the Crown Plaza Wuzhou in Beijing. This massive hotel overlooks the Bird's Nest (Beijing National Stadium) where the Summer Olympics took place just a couple of months earlier.

I have been in the Middle Kingdom for a week now to try to close a deal with the Chinese government. The lack of progress has stressed me out to no end.

It is 5:20 AM, and a brutal noise wakes me up. Instantly, a killer hangover caused by last night's dinner negotiations with the Chinese customer grips me. It is still dark outside, befitting the black mood which settles over me like a cruel contraption. I feel the familiar longing for a drink, even this early in the morning.

I realize that the phone in my hotel room is ringing, and I can sense it has been for some time. The rude awakening makes my heart palpitate. The muscles in my chest contract, and I have a hard time breathing. A familiar anxiety takes hold, worsened by the dark blue feeling of being very far from home.

When I finally bring myself to pick up the phone, I try to speak, but nothing comes out. My throat is very dry. I hear my sister call out my name in an alarming voice. She sounds very nearby, and for a moment, I think she is here in China, rather than back in Europe.

A deep premonition makes my aorta pulsate down to my stomach. I have a metallic taste in my mouth as if I had been drinking mercury or lead last night. Maybe I had.

My sister tells me our mother is dead.

I go to pieces. The voice of my sister trails off, and, similar to a nuclear meltdown, my stress chemicals reach the boiling point. I close my eyes, and I have the very real sensation of accelerating, without brakes, down a slope into an unforgiving wall. Raw panic rolls in and deepens, until suddenly my mind seems to reach escape velocity, and it goes out of orbit.

My consciousness shifts to a lower stratum and my deeper instincts take over to preserve the self. No fight or flight, but freeze. Like an animal that stands still so that its predator will not see it, I go into a state of stupor in order not to lose my mind. I no longer participate in the process of thinking and feeling. I become a detached observer.

Lying still on the bed in the pitch-dark hotel room, breathing shallow, I see myself at the age of five, walking hand in hand with my mother in the freezing cold of a winter wonderland. Our feet make crispy noises on the snow. Everything around us is silent, honoring this moment.

I feel enveloped in my mother's mystery and secure in her blessing. A precocious child, I am eager to learn, and my mother readily answers all my questions. My world is centered on her; I conform to her. There is no visible cause for concern, yet I am terrified of losing her. Separation anxiety has me overwhelmed and, in fact, so has existential fear. They say that by the age of five, you very much understand the human condition. Well, I did. I emerged from the age of innocence with a hard-and-fast grasp of the concept of death. The terror of the realization that I was mortal literally took my breath away.

Deep down, I could not believe that I could die. I had just started to learn about the world, full of symbolic meaning, and my place in it. I was a unique creature with cosmic significance. I had a contribution to make. I was good at being me and getting better every day. Surely it would be a cruel joke for me to have to die. This tragic destiny would befall lesser souls, but me?

My mother had me at forty-two. It had been an unplanned pregnancy after a very dark episode when my parents lost a son with the same name. Even today I still cannot believe that simple fact. My parents gave me my dead brother's name. No pressure.

As a replacement child, I carried the burden of my parents' unresolved sorrow. I had difficulty finding my real self, as my primary function was to be the container for the soul of my dead brother.

Very early on it was imprinted on me that I was an unexpected gift of life, my parents' last-born, precious and treasured. I was the improbable late offspring. Whether spoken out loud or not, I remember the words: *What are the odds of conceiving at the age of forty-two and having a healthy and gifted son? We need to protect him with our life.*

I later realized that this over-shielding had prevented me from accessing my own powers.

I started in life by walking on air, not on solid ground. A charmed beginning for sure, because I had escaped from the dangers of my mother's late pregnancy. It seemed to me that just by being born, I had used up my fair share of luck, and going forward, the odds were severely against me. Whatever happened next, I should not be separated from my mother.

The very same mother who was dead now.

I am a grown man in a Beijing hotel room, but I feel like I am that five-year-old boy again, walking at the hand of his mother, holding on to her for dear life. *For dear life*—the irony of that is not lost on me.

The fact that she's gone hurts like nothing has hurt before. I am now forced to think the unthinkable. This means that I too can and will die, the end of a myth that only I still believed in.

I am alone while the sun comes up over another day in China's capital. I will take the long flight back home to go and bury my mother. And I will talk to my father and my siblings, really talk, and we will feel better.

Because we are alive.

I can still love my mother, even now she's gone. That I was given the same name as my dead brother, I decide to consider a gift of devotion, highly unsettling as it has been on my journey to this day.

I feel like a lifelong spell has been lifted. I am still here even though my mother is not. Through all the pain, I feel restoration and new possibilities. This purgation of childish emotions has set me on a new path forward.

I am my own man now.

CHAPTER 8

ON THE OFF-CHANCE

BY WINTER BAER

For as long as I can remember, I've been furious with my father because of his drinking. There's just nothing good to be said about his addiction to alcohol; there's only a wave of rage deep inside me for his tragic fallibility.

For the longest time, I've hated him for what he has done to this family. I've always found it incredibly disappointing that he decided to give in to alcohol at a time when we needed him most.

As a fourth-year medical student, I know, of course, that alcoholism is a disease of the brain as well as a physical dependency, yet I still cannot comprehend how my father allowed his control over the bottle to become so completely and utterly impaired.

I know what it means to have strength of will. I strictly monitor what I eat and drink because that makes me feel powerful and in control. It seems to me that drinking alcohol does exactly the opposite. It makes you lose control of your mental and bodily functions. I fail to understand why somebody would do that to themselves.

Especially for someone like him, who is used to managing scores of people on the job, it's quite ironic that the one person he cannot seem to manage is himself.

I remember when his drinking got completely out of control, about five years ago now. It was right when my personal struggles with anorexia nervosa deepened and descended on the family like a black cloud of misery. It had started innocently enough, with my refusing to eat high-fat foods because I wanted to be as slim as some of my friends. But before I knew it, I lost myself in a compulsive controlling of my calorie intake as a way to keep in check my lingering insecurities and my pressure to be perfect.

At the lowest point, I had to be admitted into an emergency room and be force-fed by tube because my body mass index had dropped below fifteen. I can still picture a thin, emaciated version of myself lying in that hospital bed, staring at the doctor holding a clipboard with my name on it: *Winter Baer.* I will never forget how intensely I hated giving up control over my food intake to that doctor person in his white lab coat.

Possibly that is why I decided to become a doctor myself, to never again lose control like that.

In any case, my parents stood by my side for many years until I finally pulled through. But then something broke in my dad. I realize it's been a heavy burden watching his daughter trying to self-destruct, but surely a man like him should be strong enough to make it through an episode like that. Especially my dad, the superhero of my younger years. Superheroes do not start drinking when times get tough.

And yet, strangely enough, my father seemed to give up on any attempt to hold back on the booze at the very moment that I started to gain ground on the anorexia. He had always been a steady drinker, but now all restraint went out of the window. He literally drank from dawn to dusk.

Sometimes when I saw him at eight in the morning, I could tell he'd been at it already. His eyes looked watery and red, and I could almost sense his pounding headache caused by his permanent hangover.

His poison of choice was white wine, always white wine. And he did not even try to hide it; he just said the urge to drink was stronger than he was. He couldn't stop. I remember the tears in his eyes when he told my mother those exact words: "I am unable to stop, Laura. Help me."

I despised that weakness in him.

While my relationship with my father deteriorated, all of this made my bond with my mother stronger over the years. I always admired how she dealt simultaneously with his condition and mine with dignity and optimism. They almost divorced at some point, although my mother always refused to talk about it. I did not ask.

Fast forward to last Friday, when I arrived home from college for spring break and my father came up to my room to say hello. It had been ages since he had come to my room because I'd made it clear a long time ago that my room was my sanctuary and I would not be disturbed there under any circumstances.

After some uneasy small talk, my father announced that he was ready to give up drinking completely. He said he'd been sober for three months and he had every intention to stay that way. My skeptical look must have startled him because it brought a pained expression to his face. I don't know what kind of reaction he had expected from me. What you see is what you get—that's me.

Of course I wanted to believe him, more than anything. But his track record wasn't good. The odds were seriously against him. As a doctor-to-be, I had become rather cynical when it came to promises by addicts. But he certainly seemed sincere, as if he had made a life-changing decision and he wanted me to know about it. And I had to admit that he looked good, more fit and healthy than I'd seen him in a long time.

Still, he had shown good intentions before. And that did not keep him from relapsing on all previous occasions. And yet, something felt different this time, more authentic.

When he left my room, I started to explore the concept of a sober dad, and I had to admit I liked it. It would be a game-changer for all of us.

In fact, it would be the best news ever. I don't care about the money he brings in with his high-level job and his traveling all around the globe. I don't need to live in this grand mansion on the lake. I just want my dad back.

I decided I was prepared to give him my love and support on the off-chance that he could make it this time. I was so scared that he would disappoint us again.

CHAPTER 9

SPIRALING DOWN

BY CATHERINE LAVORTER

Nine days later, an agitated Peter was sitting opposite me. Just back from a trip to India, he seemed super-edgy. I carefully tested the waters.

"Welcome back. How are you today?"

He was clearly not in the mood for any pleasantries. "Here's the thing. I have to tell you about a panic attack I had on my flight back from Mumbai yesterday. It scared the hell out of me, and I do not scare easily." He was sitting on the edge of his seat.

"It started shortly after take-off. All of a sudden, I couldn't breathe. I tried to calm myself down, but the only thing I could think of was that there was no escape. I was stuck in a large, aluminum tube together with three hundred other passengers. I felt trapped, like an animal in a cage."

"Do you recall what started the anxiety attack?" I asked.

His body language showed real distress when replaying the event in his mind's eye. "A deep sense of foreboding came over me. Out of the blue, just like that. No external trigger whatsoever."

"Go on."

"We were steadily climbing to cruising altitude when this blind panic hit me. I even unbuckled my seat belt, as if leaving the plane was actually an option. A flight attendant had to tell me to sit back down and buckle up. She seemed alarmed at first, but when she saw my anxiety was real, she switched to a caregiver mode. She was probably used to people panicking now and then."

"You said it felt like you couldn't breathe. This sensation of suffocation—tell me about it."

He held a hand to his chest. "My lungs did not seem to fill with air, no matter how deeply I tried to breathe. For a moment, I thought that the cabin air was low on oxygen. I was sure I would black out any minute, up there, in mid-air. But then I noticed that people around me seemed fine, and the oxygen masks weren't dropping or anything. So I quickly concluded that air quality could not be the problem."

He took a deep breath, reliving the moment. "Anyway, I closed my eyes, and, after a while, I succeeded in calming myself down. I don't actually know how I managed to do that."

"If you could face that raw panic again, right now, what would you see and feel?"

Surprisingly, he could answer without any further deliberation. I guess it meant he had experienced this fright with all his senses.

"The color of that wave of panic would be a dark blue hue, just a shade short of black. And it comes with an ice-cold feeling of not belonging, of no longer being welcome in this world. It feels uncanny, like an urgent and primal threat that can't be denied."

He grimaced and swallowed. "It is hard to put it in exact words. It felt like a kind of hopelessness, a feeling that all was lost. Just by telling you now, I get goosebumps all over again, as if death brushes by."

There it was again—it had not taken him long to make the link with his simmering death anxiety.

"Interesting choice of words. I strongly believe your bout of panic was brought on by what we discussed last time, your fear of all things ending, of transiency coupled with an apparent lack of purpose in your life. Does that ring true?"

He was silent, so I continued. "Could it be that yet another long-haul flight meant the clock was ticking, bringing you closer to the end? Could it be that you felt guilty for wasting all this precious time just sitting on a plane?"

He stood up and started pacing back and forth in my office. "Not sure—the sensation was so frightening that, in a reflex, I asked the hostess for a gin-and-tonic to calm my nerves. Once I realized what I had done, it took all my resolve to correct it and ask for just a glass of water and some aspirin."

I could not believe what I had just heard. This was significant.

"Peter. Did you hear what you just said? Trapped on an airliner over the Atlantic, in the midst of a severe panic attack, you only had to keep silent, and a caring cabin attendant would have brought you the alcoholic drink you had ordered to do away with your fears. And yet you turned around and resisted that deep urge. That is great progress!"

He tried to suppress a smile when it dawned on him that, indeed, this had not been a small feat.

"It sure was the closest I have come to drinking since I left the safety of rehab. I did not take the bait. I resisted. Something really strong held me back, a heartfelt commitment to stay sober. I should take some pride in that, I guess. But at the same time, I have mixed feelings about the whole incident."

"Not only pride," I said. "Reassurance that your sobriety is becoming robust enough to withstand a serious breach of your equanimity, like the one you just experienced on the plane. You showed real stamina."

He still could not unconditionally accept this as progress. "Alright, but I need us to prevent these panic attacks from happening again. My job requires me to commute continuously between Europe and Asia, and the last thing I can afford now is fear of flying. My bosses would simply not understand."

"I am sure the problem is not the flying; you have been doing that all of your adult life." I wanted to be very clear. "No, I believe you need to find peace with what you aptly called the 'groundlessness' of life. There are many people who find the lack of foundation, the chimerical nature of existence, hard to bear. Again, you are not alone in this. Many talk about living in a dream or being on a rollercoaster ride when describing the experience of life. They feel the sense that anything can happen, that there is no certainty, no closure also."

Peter sat back down. "I can relate," he said. "I often have trouble distinguishing between things that really happened as opposed to something I dreamed or imagined. The day after, there doesn't seem to be a great difference between the memory of a fact, a fantasy, or a dream. They all seem equally evanescent. What's gone, is gone. How can I be certain of anything?"

I was amazed, yet again, by his apparent need to overthink things.

"Life seems an elaborate illusion at times," I said. "And some of us feel as though we have arrived here by fluke, by mistake rather than by design. For people like you, who want to be in control, that causes anxiety. It can feel like there is quicksand all around you."

"Yes, it does feel that way."

"But the fact that you are here today, talking to me about this, means that you are ready to see your own existence as absolutely fundamental. Try to see that you are life itself, you are the deep-down essence of all that is. You do not need to look outside yourself for meaning—you are it."

I waited for a minute, while he processed what I had said. "It strikes me that you are still very much identified with your mind. You believe you are the sum total of your thoughts and emotions, do you not?"

"What else would I be, then? My thoughts and feelings make me what I am, no?"

"Your mind has been conditioned by your past, by everything that happened to you since you were a little child. By what your parents and teachers told you. And let us not forget the church, since you mentioned you went to school at a Jesuit college, right?"

"Right, and that is why I now hate God. They ruined that for me."

I could relate to this, as I had many patients with the same disgust for dogmatic thinking. "Your anger is justified. Their brand of so-called religion has nothing to do with true spiritualism, it is nothing but pure doctrine. But do you see my point about you not equaling your mind? Your ego is just an outer shell, constructed to cope with the external world and its challenges as you perceive them. There is so much more to you than your persona."

Peter looked like he needed more time for this, so I decided to leave it, for now.

"Tell me this: After you had written the story about Conny, you said that writing enabled you to reach into a pool of consciousness. Well, I strongly believe that writing to you is a forceful gateway to your spiritual dimension. Like singing or painting can be an artist's door to the soul. Next time you find yourself on a plane and in danger of losing your cool, just start writing."

He seemed to find new energy when thinking of his rediscovered passion for writing. "Sure. Like that story I wrote about the death of my mother, it felt like a secret valve opened, and all these bottled-up emotions could finally escape. The release felt enormous, like I could at long last let go of my mother's hand."

"That story was multi-layered and full of overtone," I said. "It was about your mother, and about death, but also so much more than that. I had not been aware you had lost a brother by the same name."

"Since he died before I was born, technically I did not lose him," he said. "And yet, all my life, I have been aware that I have been replacing him at some level. But only now, by writing that story, did it become explicit, out in the open. And I guess I am okay with it now."

I wanted to loop back to the writing. "I encourage you to let your creative spirit roam free when you write your next story. Do not feel confined to one storyline; dare to associate freely. The strict boundaries you set yourself in daily life—they seem to fall away when you write."

"I understand what you're trying to do, and I am grateful that you're trying to inspire me, I really am. But I have to stop you, as I have the feeling we are not quite there yet. Like I said earlier, I have these dark thoughts. I feel I need to come clean with you about a destructive side of me."

"You can tell me everything," I said. "This is a safe place, remember. It is okay to take risks."

He looked down at the floor while speaking, as if suddenly deeply ashamed. "The three years before I finally had myself committed into rehab was absolute hell for me, and also for my family. I got totally lost. I did things I deeply regret now. I descended into a bottomless pit over the course of those thirty-six terrible months."

"What started that descent?" I asked.

"All these years of drinking, all the way back since my college days, I had the illusion of keeping the beast under control by counting my daily intake of alcohol. I counted the bottles of beer and the glasses of wine."

I nodded him to go on.

"That daily number of units increased steadily over the years, but I never lost count. Every night, when I went to bed, I knew exactly what I had consumed."

This was remarkable.

"Obviously, I was growing increasingly worried by the amount I drank, and I made countless resolutions to wind it down. But as long as I knew exactly how many units each day, it seemed to me, in my warped way of thinking, that I could still go back to normal. I had not yet reached a point of no return, and I could always dial back the daily count."

Now I understood what he was saying. This twisted way of reasoning, of course, was very typical for the addictive mind. "This is nothing to be ashamed of, Peter. The mind of an alcoholic can be extremely resourceful, as we both know too well. So what happened? What made you really go all out?"

"I remember it was the winter I became very worried about Wolf. He was sixteen back then, and he had been experimenting with cannabis. His school work had deteriorated fast, and he had started to hang out with the wrong type of friends."

It was visibly painful for him to tell me this. I encouraged him to go on. "I felt very guilty because it was abundantly clear that I had no hold over him. Whenever I told him to straighten out, he just answered that I was drinking way too much, so who was I to speak? I had no authority whatsoever over him. It was frustrating as hell."

Not at all surprised by this, I said, "That was some harsh and opportunistic logic on Wolf's part, but, of course, understandable from where he was standing. Those words must have shaken you up?"

"I felt terrible," he said. "And my wife Laura, of course, resented my drinking even more than before, because now it had direct repercussions on our son's future. I remember thinking, *I need to stop—I absolutely need to stop now.*"

"But you didn't?"

"I swear I could not. I just was not able to stop. Every time I tried stopping for a couple of hours, the immediate shock of withdrawal was so bad it made me lunge for a drink. I felt totally defeated. And strangely enough, that frustrating episode with my son made me let go of my golden rule of counting my daily units."

"So Wolf's telling you to drink less had the reverse effect. Rather than forcing you to stop, it triggered a full-blown alcoholic spiraling down?"

Peter's face showed anguish. "It's hard to admit that, but yes, I completely lost it. I stopped counting. I started pouring wine as if it was the source of eternal life. When one bottle was finished, I opened the next one. No more boundaries left. All bets were off."

He took a sip from his glass of water as if, even now, the simple act of drinking was still important to calm him down.

"It went downhill from there for a long thirty-six months. Finally, I came to a point where I seriously considered killing myself. I was well on my way to drinking myself to death, anyway. The thought of simply getting it over with, driving my car into a tree or buying a gun and pulling the trigger became increasingly appealing. I often traveled to places, like Russia, where it was easy to buy a gun."

I touched his arm gently. "Go on."

"Barely able to keep a focus on the job, I found myself in Moscow on business. This was early December, and it was freezing cold over there. Normally I would not think of going to Russia in the dead of winter because it is snowed under. Was it a real business reason that made me decide to go to that place, or was it fate? I still do not know."

He paused and then said, "Fact is, at some point during that week, I went into a large Russian bank on Prospect Mira near my hotel Cosmos, and exchanged two thousand five hundred Euros into Rubles. That very same evening, I had a shady local business associate take me to a local bar known for its black market dealings in handguns and other contraband. I still remember the bar's name, Crazy Daisy, infamous for its many beautiful girls dancing on the tabletops and bar. I never felt so desperate in my life as when I sat down on that bar stool and ordered a vodka."

The twist of events in his story worried me. The idea that a smart, sophisticated business man like him would be desperate enough to go to a dark mafia bar in one of the most dangerous cities in the world proved once more that addiction can drive any of us to do crazy things.

"Peter, you show real courage in telling me this. This is a side of you that you are maybe not too proud of. So what happened?"

"I finally got hold of the gun in exchange for the cash, and I took it back to my hotel room."

I gasped for breath. The thought of him with a weapon, alone in a hotel room in the Russian metropolis, sent shivers down my spine.

He spoke without emotion. "I did not switch on the light in my room. I just loaded the gun and placed it on the bed. Then I took a seat near the window. I remember staring intermittently outside into the night sky and back at the gun, contemplating living or dying." He took a deep breath. "I just sat there in the dark, slowly drinking the cheap Russian wine I had picked up on my way back to the hotel. I remember it was vile, and it took me hours to finish that bottle, while normally I had to slow myself down."

I kept quiet. The moment felt so sacred, so vulnerable that words could only do harm.

"At some point much later, I watched the sun come up above Moscow's many church roofs. I suddenly realized I was holding the gun in my hand." He looked straight at me. "I've never felt so alone and scared in my life as in that instant. I had no way out. Or . . . there was only one way out, and that was to use the gun. I actually raised it and turned it toward me, pointing it straight between my eyes. I held it with both my hands, and I was shaking heavily. And then something snapped inside of me."

I did not speak but nodded that he could tell me.

"I suddenly felt this was very wrong. I did not hear a voice from above or anything like that. I just profoundly and emotionally knew this was not the way to go out." He paused for just a moment. "That was all I needed. An incredible relief came over me when I lowered the gun."

Exhaling the breath I had held in, I said, "Sounds to me that was your rock-bottom moment, darker even than the night you had to go down to the kitchen and drink. It seems to me this was a real collapse of the ego. You came clean with yourself right there. What did you do?"

"I took the bullets out, wrapped the gun in a paper bag with the empty bottle of wine, and placed it in the garbage disposal outside the hotel. Then I went and booked myself on the first flight home."

"You never told your wife this?"

"No, I do not want her to know that I am capable of going to these extremes."

I had to come to his defense, as he himself did not. "But you did not pull the trigger. In the depths of your despair, you chose to live."

"That is correct. After I had put down the gun, the whole episode started to feel like a purge. The mortal fear I had felt when trying to turn the gun on myself gave me real momentum. I knew I had to propel myself into recovery. Procrastination was no longer an option. So I turned around and booked myself into rehab for the first time ever." He chuckled and said, "You want to hear something funny, Doc? Do you know what I came up with? A while before the Moscow thing, I had read a story about a 'comfortable but effective detox' at a luxury rehab retreat on Curacao, the island where the affluent go to kick the habit in the comfort of good food, the Caribbean sun, and the best shrinks money can buy. So I booked myself there for a four-week treatment at the Jellinek Retreat, the paradise amongst rehabs."

"Something in your tone tells me that this may not have been the best choice of cure. Which is why, probably, it was just the first one in a series of rehabs."

He looked up at the clock and saw that our hour was up. "Very true. But the place made me come to some important conclusions about the rest of my life."

CHAPTER 10

ANGST

BY PETER BAER

Christmas Day. I find myself swimming in the Caribbean Sea, an hour before dusk. I am wondering what will happen if it gets completely dark. I am pretty far out, and nobody knows where I am.

I am on Curacao, for a thirty-day rehab at the Jellinek Retreat, my first serious attempt at sobriety. This is typical of me, this coming to an exotic place to get sober. Believing that the tropical sun can take the pain away, looking for the path of least resistance. Paying a lot of money so the extra guilt will propel me forward.

I am 276 hours sober now, but I am the only one counting. It's my fight, my demons.

The water is surprisingly warm, causing sensory confusion in my brain, which is absurdly visualizing a white Christmas.

While I am putting an ever wider distance between myself and the beach, it occurs to me that it is completely up to me whether I continue swimming to open sea or not. Nobody will tell me to turn around and swim back to shore. It makes me weary to think of this complete freedom to either live or die. I feel utterly alone and groundless, literally as well as metaphorically. Can it be that I am completely unobserved?

I did not create myself, yet I am stuck with me. If I am part of the universe, why does it not care?

I shiver despite the warmness of the water.

For some reason, I see Edvard Munch's *The Scream* in my mind, the iconic painting of the hopeless figure grasping its cheeks in dread along a Norwegian fjord. I am guessing this pops up now because on the plane over, I read in the *Wall Street Journal* that the painting has just been sold for one hundred million dollars at Sotheby's in London.

While swimming, I get an image of a fifteen-year-old me, looking at that painting for the very first time in art class, and being told by the teacher that it depicts existential fear. I remember her using the German word *angst* to describe the emotion of the character in the picture. The younger me listens, fascinated both with that word and the art. I remember that evening looking up the word *angst* and wondering what 'intense inner turmoil' really meant.

Nothing is ever a coincidence.

Angst perfectly describes the loneliness and frailty I feel here in the ocean. I feel more self-conscious than I want to be. I picture myself in a Google Maps kind of way, a small red dot in a vast blue body of water. A mortal creature in a brutal cosmos. This is not a new feeling. Since I was a boy, I have always been more aware of the absurdity of it all, like I was missing a basic map of the land. Surely there must be a point to all this? And that point cannot be my swimming further out and then drowning here today.

All my life, I have been waiting for an outside power to give me direction. I have been roaming around, circling in a holding pattern above my life, counting down for it to begin.

I am way too far out now. Like a shipwrecked person, I am looking for something to hold on to. My mind's eye sees a raft. If I have not come imprinted with the right operating system, I can build one myself. I can create an essence out of my own existence. I realize that how I solve my inborn desire for meaning directly affects the quality of my life.

I suddenly feel I am back in control. I will aim high. I will aim for the meaning of my life. I feel an exhilaration with this new insight, a surge of power from a center that was off limits until this very moment.

I decide to swim back to shore. It does not end here, not today.

CHAPTER 11

RE-ENTRY

BY CATHERINE LAVORTER

Peter and I found ourselves sitting on the terrace outside my office, overlooking Lake Geneva. It was a cold but bright January morning, and I had invited him to join me outside for a breakfast session, complete with croissants and espresso a la Suisse.

The morning sun, shining down on the frozen lake and its banks with their elevated vineyards, made for a magnificent view. From where we were sitting, we could see all the way up to the Chateau de Morges, a magnificent castle set in its own park. In springtime, the one-hundred-and-fifty-thousand tulips and daffodils surrounding the castle would bloom. But for now, the tall chestnut trees above the castle took the eye even higher, where the great Mont Blanc towered above all the other mountain peaks.

It's quite funny when you think of it, the fact that our addiction-centric healing facility is located in the midst of the most famous wine-tasting houses in the Lake Geneva region. I guess it means we're not hiding from temptation, but rather willfully facing it.

Despite the breathtaking Alpine backdrop to our rendezvous, Peter looked disheartened. I knew he had just come back from a short break to the Tuscan countryside with his wife, Laura, so I had kind of expected him to be reinvigorated. It had been their first time out alone as a couple since his release from rehab.

This was not good.

Sipping on his Lavazza espresso, Peter looked at me and said, "This is fabulous coffee. Bitter and not too rich, just the way I like it. Thanks for having this meeting in the open air. It makes for a welcome break from sitting in an office. Or on a plane, for that matter."

I was pleasantly surprised to hear him say these words. He was clearly making an effort to do a little song and dance before plunging into deeper, more serious dialogue. Usually, he did not bother with small talk and often skipped these first few rungs on the ladder of conversation. But today he did, and I appreciated his willingness to invest in the relationship, despite his apparent somber mood.

I matched his tone, "It's my pleasure. With a wonderful winter sun like this, it would be a shame for us to stay inside. And this view never fails to cheer me up. Now tell me: How was the time alone with Laura? It must have been good to give each other some undivided attention after the turbulence of the last few months."

He hesitated, and I got a clear sense that talking about the weekend was disturbing. Looking out across the lake, I could barely hear when he spoke. "I think Laura and I both had very high expectations for this trip to begin with. I guess we had hoped we could just copy and paste some of the really great journeys we did together in the early days, before my drinking got in the way."

I waited for a moment before I answered.

"So I take it things did not go as expected. What happened?"

"Well, the weekend was bound to fail as we tried to reconstruct a romantic fantasy of the past. But boy, did reality catch up with us, there in lovely Tuscany." He sighed. "It was jarring how nostalgia for our younger years was quickly replaced by the realization that things were not going to be the same with me not able to drink. The trip made us see that the past really is irrevocable, that we both have changed and so has our marriage."

It was clear that Peter had put his mind to work again and had analyzed the Italian weekend experience to death.

As I did not want to encourage him to go further down this path, I decided to steer the discussion in another direction.

"This really is the first time we have discussed your relationship with Laura. We touched upon her disapproving of your drinking a couple of times, but I think it would be worth looking at the quality of the bond the two of you have. Do you mind giving me some background and history to your marriage before we further discuss the trip you took together?"

He stood up and walked to the edge of the terrace, near the water. I could tell my interrupting his stream of thought had upset him. I had a feeling he was not used to being directed.

"Alright, let's see. Laura and I have been married for twenty-two years this month. Our traveling to Italy was a wedding anniversary of sorts. She and I met when we were both taking a post-graduate MBA at Leuven University, the oldest college in Europe. Those were glorious times. I could talk for hours about those memories." He smiled when he said this, staring over the water. "She was the prettiest girl on campus and, if anything, she looks even more beautiful now. Anyway, we've been together ever since. The lady's got class and style. What can I say? I am very lucky."

It was sweet how he spoke about her.

"And what is she like, your wife?"

"She is the strongest person I know, a woman with real stamina. She started her own company a couple of years ago, and she is successful and independent. Together, we have battled our way through our share of very difficult situations, especially the long and many cycles of anorexia nervosa which our daughter Winter has had to fight her way through."

Silently, I was amazed that their marriage had survived the drinking and then this heinous disease on top. Anorexia is known to destroy many a family unit, as its destructive dynamic tends to intoxicate and permeate any system of people trying to battle it.

"Laura is resilient as a person, and that is the main reason she is still with me. She could have easily left me when I just about destroyed our family with my drinking. But she didn't. In fact, she gave me a strong ultimatum, and that helped me finally commit to abstinence."

I was triggered by the apparent ease by which he used the word "ultimatum." "We will come back to Laura's personality, but can you tell me more about that ultimatum. This seems relevant. An ultimatum often backfires when a person is being forced into something they didn't choose of their own free will. In the final showdown, somebody always loses."

He responded as if stung by a wasp. "No, it was nothing like that. Laura patiently waited until all else had failed before telling me that she would leave me if I did not stop drinking. She remained supportive even during the horrible last three years before I finally quit. She stood by me while I kept spiraling down as if she trusted me enough to know that things would turn eventually."

He looked at me with what appeared to be surprise. "Come to think of it, she had more faith in me than I did myself. I told you that there was a time when I was convinced I would drink myself to death, when I could no longer see a way out. Laura could have walked away right then, but instead she stood by me and carried on with her life as normally as possible, somewhat detached but still with love. Still there, present."

He paused for a moment, and then continued, clearly overtaken by emotion. "She knew very well that the ultimate decision to quit had to come from me and that forcing my hand would not help. All this time she held back, knowing that I had not yet reached that point. It is nothing less than amazing that she was willing to see it through to its bitter end. For better or for worse, as they say."

I kept silent.

"When I finally did reach rock-bottom, rather than being shocked or angry, she composed herself and told me in a straightforward manner that she would leave me if I did not take this final opportunity to stop. It was very clear that she meant it, but it was not an act of aggression or hostility, but rather of compassion. She seemed to sense that she was the ultimate catalyst, and she was right. The thought of losing her did tip the scale and gave me the final push. When willpower is totally impaired, as it was in my case, a small miracle is needed. That is what she gave me, a small miracle."

"When was this?" My voice sounded weird, as I found myself having trouble containing my own emotions.

"Well, her timing was flawless. When I was down and out, she used that desperation and told me to quit drinking once and for all. She said this was my last chance to claim her love. Quite a ruthless strategy it was, in hindsight, with a subtle feminine quality to it. In any case, it worked."

This sounded rather unorthodox and raised my suspicion. Often, power battles involving a heavy ultimatum get ugly very fast and even if the husband agrees to go into rehab to save the marriage, without fail, there would be some kind of revenge or retaliation afterward. But Peter seemed to express no hard feelings whatsoever of being strong-armed into abstinence. I was amazed by the powers attributed to Laura. It made me wonder even more what had gone wrong this past weekend.

"She sounds like a forceful person and very dedicated to you. So tell me about Tuscany."

"Ah, yes. We were staying at the Villa Campestri, a Renaissance house surrounded by olive gardens and set on a hilltop, overlooking the Mugello Valley in the Tuscan countryside. We had been there before, years ago, when things were still more or less under control."

"With hindsight, it might have been wiser to pick an entirely new location for your first trip sober. These beautiful but familiar settings you describe must have been a powerful reminder of more carefree times when you could still drink, at that exact same place."

"Very true, but too late now, obviously." He sounded vexed. I must have hit a nerve with my analysis. "Anyway, it rained in Tuscany for three days straight. This added a melancholy to the surroundings. As if the weather wanted to underscore that things have definitively changed now, and life was going to be nothing but hard for me as a recovering alcoholic, even in glorious fucking Italy. Excuse my language."

I secretly mused about his propensity to connect dots which should not be connected, like now with the rain. He often saw synchronicities, events with no causal relationship, but in his mind, they were related in a clear and meaningful way. I tried to keep a serious face. "Surely the rain was not responsible for spoiling your stay? What do you think was the main reason for your disappointment?"

"Well, let me think how I can convey to you the anticlimax Laura and I both felt. I think it is best if I tell you about one specific afternoon when we went to visit Arezzo, a Medieval town just south of Florence where we used to go to in the early days."

I had a distinctly bad feeling about them visiting old romantic getaways. "Yes, please help me understand what happened."

"Well, we had rented an Alfa Romeo Spider and drove off mid-morning to arrive there in time for lunch. Arezzo has the same old world charm as its bigger rival cities like Siena and Florence, but with fewer tourists. The many small streets and the wonderful Piazza Grande, its main square, give it that real old continent vibe."

An aficionado of Italy myself, I felt like I was right there.

"We walked around, gazing at the quaint antique shops and art galleries while looking for a nice restaurant to have lunch. It had stopped raining for a bit, and many couples took seats outside of the many bars and restaurants to enjoy the precious sunshine. Yet the more people I watched laughing and enjoying themselves, the more I felt tension and anxiety build up inside me."

"What do you think caused that?"

"My stomach was tied in knots. I felt queasy. I even had to sit down for a minute because I felt dizzy."

"I understand that is how you felt, but what do you think triggered it?" I pressed.

"To be really honest, I was overwhelmed by seeing people drink wine and have fun. Simple as that. The sensory input was just too much, and old memories and associations got the better of me. My cravings for a drink grew stronger by the minute." He added as an afterthought, "And I felt guilty."

I knew exactly what he meant, but I wanted him to say it out loud. "Guilty?"

"Yes! Hell, I was supposed to be cured. I knew Laura expected me to be my old self, the fun and romantic guy she had married twenty-two years ago. She had been looking forward to this trip for a long time; she deserved a good time. After all, I had successfully made it through rehab, and now we were together in this wonderful place, where we had been very happy in the old days. If I was not able here in Arezzo to be the Peter she remembered, where would I be?"

I could see it was painful for him to relay this to me because he knew deep inside that his argument was false. I held my breath.

He carefully concluded, "I could sense Laura's deep disappointment when I said I did not feel well. Her obvious disillusionment, although she tried to hide it from me, made me even more sick to my stomach. Things got worse from there, until eventually we decided to go back to the hotel."

Distressing as all of this was, it was time to show some tough love. "Peter, I am sorry, but, really, you should have known better. After four stints of rehab, you have experienced firsthand that re-entry into society is very difficult. Especially in the beginning, it is unrealistic and impossible to be enjoyable and entertaining in the company of others without a drink, if alcohol has been your social lubricant for so many years." I looked for an analogy. "Compare it with the re-entry of a spacecraft into Earth's atmosphere. Also, that is tricky business right there. As it re-enters the airspace, the capsule encounters violent air friction, which causes intense heat. Without insulation coating, like a heat shield, it will burn up with its crew inside, before it can land safely."

He was listening intently.

"For you to re-enter and land safely into civilization, you need to insulate yourself. You need to shield and protect yourself against friction. The requirement to be romantic and fun in places where other people consume alcohol freely is the very definition of friction for you as an alcoholic. Do you see my point?"

He stared at his feet. "I get it, Doc."

I took a minute to consider how best to take this further. "I am afraid the two of you were overly ambitious when going on this trip. From the start, it seemed designed to fall well below expectations. You went to an old and familiar place where you used to drink and enjoy life together. Believe me, the weather was not the problem." I was angry that he had allowed himself to be tricked into this unhelpful situation. "It is not uncommon for an alcoholic to sabotage his own sobriety on an unconscious level. Possibly you were setting yourself up to drink again. Maybe you were preparing yourself for relapse by showing that abstinence is incompatible with marriage?"

It was clear he had not looked at it from this angle. He seemed surprised by my anger, but I knew he needed this wake-up call.

He went on the defensive. "I am so tired of it all. I am sick of wearing a mask, of putting on this brave face as if everything is back to normal. This is not me, not yet, anyway. I am still craving for the old stuff. I am far from recovered."

"Nobody expects you to act as if everything is back to normal," I said.

"I want to come clean on the fact that I cannot drink anymore, ever. But the world doesn't seem to let me. There is temptation everywhere I look."

I could tell his logic was flawed and that he was in a fragile state. "I think I understand what you mean. Being sober now, people expect you to be 'over it.' No doubt, it is tiresome to keep up a façade, to hide your doubts and fears, and resist the cravings, of course." It did him well to find a sympathetic ear, so I continued. "Especially toward Laura, who you believe expects you now to be again the great guy she used to know and love. That is really something the two of you need to untangle, these unrealistic expectations. Because when unaddressed, they could make you drink again."

This seemed to resonate. He looked at the clock and then right back at me. "I know our time is up, but can I ask you one more thing before we finish up?"

"Sure. I realize today could not have been easy for you."

"Well, I will have to face some even harder stuff, this coming week. I am required to go to Las Vegas to attend my company's Global Sales Conference. I'm sure you can appreciate my worry because again, this is a situation where drinking is expected. It's even quasi-compulsory, you could say. I guess you know what I am talking about. Open bar every night, drinking and gambling with the guys, a long week of mandatory celebrations."

He looked desperate.

"It takes place in the world's biggest casino, for God's sake. I don't know how I will be able to get through this. People know I am back on the job, and they'll smell blood if I do not drink. It's so not part of the culture not to booze up during the sales conference. Everyone is expected to put their *work hard, play hard* hat on for a full week. Fuck."

There was a need for me here to take a formal stance as his doctor. "If there really is no way you can avoid this trip to Vegas, I need you to protect yourself. Under no condition can you be made to drink. I want you to talk to a trusted party within the company. You need to tell this person in confidence that you are in recovery and that you will want to go back to your room at times when all the others are partying. If that is not possible, then you should not go at all. I am willing to attest to that."

Peter seemed relieved and offered no resistance. "Okay. I will do that. I will talk to HR. It will just be hard to get through next week, that's all. Again, I wish I was normal."

"You know that as far as alcohol is concerned, you will never be normal again. This condition is for life. But I guarantee you that you will learn to enjoy living again. You are doing some really hard time right now, but, for sure, you'll see the payoff later."

I felt bad about sending him off like that. I wished we had spent more time on prepping him for the Vegas challenge ahead. While we were walking toward the door, I did not want him to leave empty-handed.

"And remember that writing is a door to your deeper self. You say you are tired of wearing a mask. Well, I advise you to write about Vegas. You will find this is liberating. Try not to focus on the drinking, be open and put yourself out there. Learn from the experience."

CHAPTER 12

SINGULARITY

BY PETER BAER

I've been stuck at Chicago's O'Hare International Airport for the past four hours now. The board shows only canceled flights due to a blinding blizzard raging over the Midwest. With hundreds of other weary travelers, I am gazing down on the snow-covered tarmac through the floor-to-ceiling airport windows.

It's only two PM, but the ambiance feels like early evening. This perception may be psychological in nature, because we all feel gloomy. The huge Christmas tree in the center of the old, worn-out terminal does nothing to cheer us up; everyone just wants to go home.

Outside, the fallen snow is blowing around in all directions, causing a complete whiteout. The angry wind slams snowflakes into the windows. I have plenty of time to watch the ice crystals frost the glass, with dendrites branching out in asymmetry as if to impress me with their singularity. I see the window glass turn translucent under a thin film of ice.

A familiar mix of happiness and grief engulfs me. It is said that melancholy is sadness that has taken on lightness. The sliver of joy I feel in these otherwise cheerless circumstances is triggered by the untouched, pristine snow, which has always been a symbol of bliss to me.

Waking up to unexpected snowfall was my ultimate childhood delight. It meant no school and a total breaking away from the ordinary. You could always count on snow to turn a grim world into a perfect one, to cover reality with a layer of white magic.

As a grown-up, though, there seems to be only a downside to snow. I look at the tired faces around me, and it makes me sad. I realize it's all within the confines of our heads. I bet we all have a latent desire deep down to go outside and start a mad snowball fight, but there is just no catalyst here to make that happen.

And I'm really tired.

On my way back to Europe, I have arrived here in Chicago from sunny Las Vegas, where I spent the last seven days locked up at the unavoidable Caesar's Palace as a participant in my company's annual Sales Conference.

My mind drifts back to exactly one week ago, when I arrived at the casino and stared open-mouthed at the maddening crowd who played the slot machines with one hand while holding a Budweiser in the other. Three thousand six hundred sales execs, all working for the same global software mammoth, have assembled for this big production on the Las Vegas Strip. Tribute will be paid to the illusion that, once again, this past year, we've beaten the competition. No doubt, somewhere in a similar convention center in Paris or Boston, our adversaries are doing the exact same thing. And so the world turns.

No efforts were spared to make us feel part of a global powerhouse. The facts are there. Our turnover equals the GDP of a small European country. Our CEO shakes hands at the Davos Global Forum with Chinese President Xi Jinping and German Chancellor Merkel. The value of our global brand is right up there with Google's and Apple's.

And yes, we feel proud to be here.

I admit that the incredible settings of the Gala Dinner triggered a definite pride in me to belong to this company. My colleagues and I are sitting at no less than three hundred oval tables seating twelve each, inside the world's largest ballroom. This space is so gargantuan that it is impossible to see across the room to the other side.

After a sumptuous American-styled dinner, the keynote speaker grants the Global Sales Award to Team India for persevering and reaching target despite the most severe floods in the country's long history. The crowd goes wild while Coldplay's "A Sky Full of Stars" blasts from the Herculean sound system that is also used when The Stones go on tour.

I feel the adrenaline pumping, and my hair is standing on end. I am in complete awe, and so is everyone in the room.

Tick in the box.

I've not been left alone for one minute this whole week, playing my part in a sophisticated corporate choreography. No need to question the why of things— we are in Vegas to celebrate the what. All of us are essential, yet interchangeable cogs in a global sales machine. There seems to be no room for identity; we go for safety in conformity. A large corporation is like an army: The platoon matters, not the individual.

It's funny when you think of it. Our overriding commercial objectives seem to be of a higher order than any local disputes we might have. My colleagues have flown in from fifty-two different countries to this desolate place in the middle of the Nevada desert as if participating in a Global Peace Summit in a demil-itarized zone.

Our Russian sales reps have breakfast with their American peers not discussing the annexation of Crimea. Arabs drink tea with Israelites not touching upon Gaza. Greeks and Germans play the roulette side by side, unconcerned with the next tier of Triumvirate debt relief. All of the real-world conflicts which are a burning platform outside this hotel are suspended for the duration of this grandiose ego fest.

Nothing unites people like money does, at least for one week in this Palace of Kitsch, with not one single window to the world. Narrowing our perspectives down to our trading targets has us properly fixated and acting as brothers-in-arms. The plot in Vegas indeed is to make us feel like corporate warriors. This is cleverly crafted because once we are in that frame of mind, you can ask us anything. Sales heroism is to the alpha male what cocaine is to an addict—injected straight into the vein.

The global software market is depicted as a war zone, and acts of bravery on this commercial battlefield are rewarded in a very public way. Doses of praise are doled out in the form of sales awards and entry tickets to the select line-up of the President's Club.

The group is split in two. A minority who "made Club" and those who did not. The quota-achieving elite will go with their spouses on a lavish company-paid vacation to Cabo, Mexico. The others will do what it takes to make it next year or will die trying. In any case, the President's Club puts a strain on quite a few marriages as the spouses at home urge their husband on.

All of this is pretty addictive stuff, taking place in a casino, of all places. It has us all hooked in an eerie, primeval way. And God knows that I am prone to anything compulsive. The company is very clever about it.

The art of selling is framed in terms of strategies, campaigns, and tactics. Recognition is structured as a system of ceremonies, rites, and rituals, appealing directly to the brainstem, the oldest part of our intellect where primitive instincts and primal emotions overrule more sophisticated reasoning.

Our reptilian brain took millions of years to develop, and its agenda is to assure we survive and thrive. It can make us reach beyond our boundaries, fueled by its potent will to power. Think of the ritual behavior of two lions establishing territories and competing for dominance. Not unlike two sales execs going after the same deal. Winner takes it all. Brilliant set-up and a proven concept borrowed from the world of predators.

Amongst the thousands of sales colleagues, only very few are female, and the ladies really stand out. Obviously, they are aware of the 200:1 ratio here at the event and bask in the extraordinary attention. Dressed for success in Giorgio Armani business suits and spectacular Bulgari evening dresses, they work their double magic of beauty and brains.

A few really stand out. There is Sarah from Detroit, Ana from Sao Paulo, and, of course, Viktoriya from St. Petersburg, who wins over the crowd while presenting a customer success story in broken English with an irresistible Russian accent. I suspect she masters the

English language far better than this, but she uses her thick Russian articulation for maximum effect on the sea of male onlookers in the plenary session, and it works. The crowd loves it.

She is flawless, both in style and essence. Her particular Russian blend of girlish charm and business savvy is a winning combination with this hard-to-please wolf pack. I can only imagine what she can accomplish with a customer. Viktoriya and the other women radiate personality, in stark contrast with the men here. I've been observing my male colleagues during the week, and they all seem cast in the same mold.

Look at the men, and you see ardent crusaders, equipped with adequate body armor, business casual, no tie. They are cool and composed in their personas and robust in their convictions. Life is straightforward, without room for doubts or regrets. Or any other feelings, for that matter. Or so it looks. But I know from experience that fear is a powerful emotion in sales people.

Internal competition makes us far more nervous than the customer does. We are afraid to get behind our peers on the leader board, to miss quota, and, ultimately, to get fired. And these worries overlay a dread buried even deeper, the trepidation of rejection from a top-selling sales culture that provides not only our livelihood but also our self-esteem. To be in sales is in effect an elaborate immortality project, feeding off our basic survival instinct.

We can achieve greatness amongst our peers and feel part of a symbolic system that provides us with a sense of accomplishment, not to mention cash in our pockets. No need for command-and-control. We so much want to be part of this that we act under our own steam. Despite my earlier reservations about this whole set-up, I feel pumped.

I can't help but wonder, though, what the others see when they look at me. I am sure my polished exterior cannot hide the fact that my inner weather is more unstable than theirs. And my newfound sobriety makes me even more doubtful of my abilities. Or could it be that my peers are in the same constant state of flux as I am? Could it be that they are less sure of themselves than they appear on the face of things?

Maybe so. How else could I have stood my ground for so long in this competitive crowd and even managed to climb up the food chain? And I'm one of only a handful of colleagues not touching alcohol. Is this not a competitive advantage, rather than a handicap?

For the first time ever, it strikes me that there is absolutely no way that I'd be somehow unique, with my shifting emotions and constant mind chatter. I concede that all of us must have this same inner dialogue going on. I almost laugh out loud at the thought of speech bubbles floating above all the heads of the conference audience. Hundreds of personal narratives going on at the same time. I feel instant relief just by visualizing this.

The seemingly superhuman equanimity of this group could very well be only skin-deep, and it no longer intimidates me. Our singularity may be hidden, like a tattoo beneath our Hugo Boss shirts, but it is there. If anything, I'm sure of that now. I realize that I have my newfound sobriety to thank for seeing things as they really are.

I come back to the here and now at O'Hare in Chicago, when from the corner of my eye I notice the flight board jump from reds to greens. My fellow travelers are picking up their bags and moving to the gates with restored spirits.

I must have been standing here for quite a while, lost in thought, because I see now that the sky has cleared outside. The ice crystals on the window glass reflect the rays of a pale winter sun. Crews outside are finishing the de-icing of the wings of the planes. We are back on the move.

I feel as if a weight has been lifted off my shoulders. Sales is a game, and I am a seasoned player. But it is no more than a game. It is not who I am. And the others are no robots but flawed human beings, just like me. Also, for the first time in quite a while, I allow myself to be proud of my abstinence. I did it. I did not have a drink this whole damned week, even in that Godforsaken watering hole in the middle of the Nevada desert.

My mood gets a further lift when I hear Bruce Springsteen's "Dancing in the Dark" play in the background. The video wall projects the classic 1984 clip in which The Boss invites a young and stunning Courteney Cox to join him to dance on stage, her first shot at fame.

I look at the "Now Boarding" sign next to my flight. I walk up to the gate and feel lighthearted while I show my boarding pass to the cute blond attendant. Her name tag spells "Vicky," which instantly reminds me of my charming St. Petersburg colleague. This Vicky smiles back at me in a professional yet personal way. I am sure she is genuinely happy to see me and is not pretending.

CHAPTER 13

FEAR OF LIVING

BY CATHERINE LAVORTER

Adaline Vikander, a Ph.D. student of mine at the Psychology Department of Geneva University, sat in as an observer on the next therapy session with Peter. The young woman looked striking in a tight, yet somewhat short navy skirt and a buttoned-up white blouse and high heels. She wore dark-rimmed glasses and with her blond hair pulled back in a bun, she looked slightly sexier—in a bookish kind of way—than I considered appropriate.

Seeing Peter's first reaction, I could not help but wonder whether she would distract all of my male patients this way, unintentionally, of course. I made a mental note to talk to her about the dress code. We should take the "sexy secretary" look down a notch for the sake of professionalism.

I had invited Miss Vikander to sit in, not only to help her finish the internship part of her post-graduate academic trajectory, but also because she was a certified meditation coach. She and I had talked for many hours about the benefits of yoga and mindfulness to complement traditional addiction-related therapy. And I had a feeling that Peter would be greatly helped by this combination.

"First of all, about your Vegas story. You took me with you, all the way to Caesar's Palace. The way you described the manipulative and intricate ways of a big corporation, I felt I was totally there, part of the crowd. However, I could tell you were not really connecting with others on any meaningful level, other than business. Is that correct?"

Pulling his gaze away from Miss Vikander, Peter turned to face me.

"Mm, yes, but I was not looking to connect with anyone. I was in self-protection mode, as you told me to be. The easiest way for me to do that was to switch my personality features to their corporate settings."

I could not help but laugh.

"That's quite funny, and fascinating. How do you do that, exactly?"

He addressed me in a more formal way than he usually did, probably to show his respect for me in the presence of my trainee.

"I find that focusing on professional matters helps to push out my obsessive thoughts about drinking and also my deeper concerns about life in general. The sterile concepts and best practices of business act as contaminants."

"In what way?"

"Well, I find that buying and selling have an elegant precision to it. The stakes of the game are clear, and I will make damn sure that I am on the winning side of the equation. So, yes, whenever I need it, I can enter this whole parallel universe which I control and master." He thought for a moment and added a witticism, typical of him. "Life becomes a spreadsheet."

Both Adaline and I had to smile at this, which he clearly enjoyed. He took a sip of water and continued. "I realize, of course, that this world of commerce is nothing but a fake empire."

"What do you mean by that?"

"Sorry, I should explain. I am a fan of Brooklyn band The National, and 'Fake Empire' is one of their signature songs. It's about a generation lost to disillusion, young people who cannot deal with day-to-day reality and decide to pretend that the world is full of magic. Much like the make-believe microcosm I was a part of in Vegas."

"I see. But despite the fakeness of it, you seem at home in the realm of big business?"

"What I like is that it holds no secrets for me, unlike life itself, I should say. The continuous flow of business transactions makes me feel like I am in control of my destiny. Or at least it is a sweet and welcome illusion." As an afterthought, he added, "When I am in selling mode, I feel liberated, because the rules of the game are clear and transparent, not opaque as they are in real life."

I took a moment to let this sink in. I looked sideways, and I saw that Adaline Vikander was furiously scribbling down notes on a legal pad.

"I would like to understand better. What do you mean when you say the rules of life are opaque?"

"Existence, to me, is erratic."

"How so?"

"When it comes to life and death, the axioms are oblique," he said. "Often, the workings of the basic principles seem incomprehensible to all but the highest experts in their domains, like neurosurgeons removing a rare brain tumor or the guys at the CERN Lab discovering the God particle to explain why you and I are able to exist. The verdicts of these pundits, even when false or destructive, are beyond question. They can play God without you and me being able to challenge them in their fields."

"In other words, life is beyond your control?"

"Exactly, and I hate that."

"You realize you have to let this urge to control go?"

He did not acknowledge this. He did not really like to be told what he should do or not do.

"You referred earlier to your deeper concerns about life," I continued. "You mean your fear of death, right?"

Peter nodded solemnly.

"Would you say that this preoccupation with death is your primary concern in life?"

He looked very alert now. I could tell this was very close to his core. He hesitated. "Yes, I would. Every morning, I wake up to yet another day without a solution to my mortality problem." He looked at me carefully, to check my expression. When he saw that I was not about to scoff at him, he continued. "Every day I realize, as if for the first time, that my life will eventually end. And every day, this weighs down on my chest, like a foot of fresh earth on top of a coffin. My coffin."

He had a faint smile on his face, but it was the smile of somebody in pain. "I know I must sound like the quintessential neurotic in a Woody Allen movie, but to me, this is very real. Most mornings, I wake up in great spirits, and I feel fine for a couple of minutes. Then this sudden terror comes over me like a tidal wave, I have no control over it. It's this morbid dread that runs deep within me."

"I can assure you that most people are at times overwhelmed by primal anxiety, but it is indeed rare to experience this constantly. Most people feel this way only when confronted with death or loss in their inner circle. Your primal fear seems to break through the cracks every morning before your defenses are intact."

He was not really listening; he was still focused on trying to convey to me the exact sentiment.

"*Fallen* is the word that best describes the sinking sensation in my stomach. I feel like Adam waking up to discover he's been thrown out of Eden. It feels inchoate, you know—like it is just the beginning of something really terrible and the worst is yet to come."

I decided to let him get it out of his system. Articulating the fear as precisely as possible is a good basis for healing.

"A circuit breaker in my brain puts a stop to all existential thinking every time it is confronted with that same contradiction: *Life instinct telling me to avoid death at all cost while my brain points out that all such effort is futile.*" He sighed. "Often, I think the whole concept of dying must be an epic misunderstanding, an unfortunate misinterpretation of some biblical allegory. Death as the unavoidable last page of the book of life? I just cannot believe that."

"Please elaborate. Why is it that you cannot accept death as a fact of life?"

"Because all my efforts to grow, my constant failing and learning from my mistakes, all of that must lead to some satisfying conclusion. I feel I am constantly preparing for something greater still to come. Dying cannot be that conclusion. I feel there should be some graduation from life, onto a higher station."

"It is clear to me that you fear to live because you fear to die. And the irony of it is that you will be able to face the prospect of death only if and when you have had the experience of fully living. Do you see the *Catch 22* you find yourself in?"

I could see him struggling to grasp the deeper meaning of what I'd said. I decided to get some outside help.

"Earlier you referred to yourself as a neurotic. Another famous psychologist, Otto Rank, said that 'The neurotic refuses the loan of life to escape the debt of death.'"

This hit home. He looked up as if he'd seen the light. "I think I get this. So how can I get rid of this paralyzing terror?"

"Well, you repress your fear of death by using a number of defense mechanisms which, in turn, restrict your freedom to live and grow as a person. I would like to explore those defenses with you."

"Okay. I like where this is going. Tell me more about these defense mechanisms."

"We all want to escape somehow from the fact that we will die," I said. "There are two modes of coping with this existential anxiety, both based upon a denial of death."

He hung onto my words.

"One type of person deeply believes in their own specialness and personal invulnerability and is convinced at an unconscious level he or she is protected from death. The other type puts their faith in the existence of an ultimate rescuer. This could take the form of a religious belief that detoxifies death, for example."

"I see. Which type am I, then?"

"I would like you to answer that. Let me ask you this: Do you feel that you control the events of your life, or do these events occur independently of your actions? In other words, do you feel you control your personal destiny?"

He took a moment to ponder my question.

"I'd like to think that I am in control of my destiny. And more and more so, as time passes."

I liked his intuitive way of approaching this topic. He was on a roll.

"The irony of life is that you get better and better at it, and you come to expect it to further spiral upwards. When you get to marry the girl you love and you have children together, when you get promoted up the corporate chain, you actually start to believe you have superpowers. That eventually you'll be able to also dodge the final bullet and get away with not dying at all."

"You have just answered your own question—about which type you are."

"Do you mean I believe I am above the fray? Nothing can touch me?"

"A person like you, oriented toward specialness as a defense mechanism for denial of death, is often a compulsive achiever, someone who wants to stand out from the crowd and has difficulties accepting their own frailties and limits."

"So my ambition on the job all these years had to do with my fear of death?"

"Yes. Your professional climb to glory, even in the capacity of a high-functioning alcoholic, has been extremely important to you in terms of an immortality project, a denial of your impermanence."

"So I think I am special, then? Reminds me of that song by Shania Twain." I could tell he was on thin ice, trying to joke his way out of a precarious topic.

"I think that, unconsciously, you believe you will not die because you think you are not like everybody else—you're special. When I say this to you, what is going through your mind?"

He was done joking. "Well, somehow, what you say rings true. My gut feeling is that I am too clever to die, that only a freak accident or an external attack could kill me. Something as prosaic as old age or sickness cannot get to me. I should just not be stupid and travel to an Ebola-infected country or buy a one-way ticket to Mars. If I respect these basic rules, I should be fine. Sounds crazy, right?"

"No, not crazy at all. It sounds unfamiliar to you because you have never made this intuitive belief explicit before."

"Wow, this does stir things up. I have a feeling we are looking at things from a new angle here. Can I tell you what I am thinking?"

Peter looked first at me and then at our trainee. Miss Vikander had been following the discussion in the background, and now she felt self-conscious because Peter seemed to address the question to the both of us.

She nodded.

I smiled and said, "Sure, go ahead."

"Well, I feel I am entitled to live. Wait, I'd like to put it even stronger: I feel it is my birthright to be alive. My dying would mean an outside force has rigged the game, because when it comes to mastering life, I am an expert."

"What do you mean by that?" I asked.

"Well, try to put a roadblock in my path, and I will find a way around it. My mind protects me by using pure logic, the most basic design code in the universe, to shield me against all the randomness that fate throws at me." He said all this with a defiant passion.

"What I hear," I responded, "is that mastery and control are very important to you, and you rely on your mind to guide you. But uncertainty is a fact of life, and we must coexist with it. Your mind cannot control what happens to you. And death, also your own, is inevitable. You will have to face that fact, eventually."

I waited for a reaction, but there was none, so I continued. "To you, thinking is the key to solving all mysteries in life. Constant thinking provides you with some relief from anxiety but also severely restricts your daily living. There is no room for spontaneity or creativity, for personal growth. There is only black-and-white logic."

"But I have always thought it was my mind that made me special."

"Your intellect is above average, Peter. What I am saying is that, often, your mind seems to control you, not the other way around."

He was listening.

"You said so earlier: When you're in a business mode, you use your mind as a sharp tool of logic, and you feel in control. But outside of your professional life, your personal mind—your ego—takes over and controls you."

He seemed reluctant to accept this, so I tried to clarify. "At all times, you should use your mind as an instrument, also outside of the professional context. Let me use an analogy. Think of your mind as if it were a car. You do not just want it to accelerate without anybody steering, right? Nothing good can come from that."

He nodded.

"You are not the car, but you are the driver of the car. By the same token, you are not your mind. You should be a detached observer of your mind and take control when needed. Don't let it carry you away." I saw this resonated, so I wanted to cement this further. "Your mind ruminates constantly. Remember the picture in Amalfi you showed me in our very first session, the one you associated with your compulsive thinking even at the age of twenty-two? You need to understand that your mind is a two-edged sword. It believes it is the boss and has the right to control you."

He was staring at the ground again, his way of processing difficult information. I could see he was considering my words carefully. "This is hard to swallow. I have always been proud of my intellectual prowess. But now I see that I am using my mind in the wrong way."

"As I said earlier, you allow your mind to overthink things and to build its own narrative. You need to de-identify from the story of you—that is not who you really are. It is just your ego talking."

In true style, he answered. "I do get wrapped up into concepts and abstractions to escape from reality. The more sophisticated the ideas and symbols I use to describe my world, the further I seem to get away from death and decay, it feels like."

"Beautifully put, Peter. But the conclusion is that you need to stop thinking. Dissociating from your mind terrifies you because it feels like you lose grip on your reality. And yet, that is the way out for you."

I saw I had to reframe this so he would understand better. "You are the victim of painful, long-lived emotions, like these primal fears which you never worked through properly. These hurtful emotions linger below the surface and trigger you to construct sophisticated intellectual systems to justify your suppressed fears. In short, we need more feeling, rather than more thinking. You need to connect with your pain—face the music, so to speak."

He looked pale in the face. This had been quite intense. It seemed only ten minutes ago that we started the session, and yet I saw the hour was up. "I need some time to digest it all. I feel exhausted."

"Sure," I said. "Do me one favor, please. In preparation for our next session, dig deeper, and question why you fixate on controlling everything with your mind. Think about a time when you broke through that illusion of control."

CHAPTER 14

TIPPING POINT

BY PETER BAER

Late November 2011. My plane touches down at Moscow's Domodedovo airport, and I fast-track through Russian border security using my frequent-entry passport. I rush past a crowd of tourists, my mind anticipating a million things that need to happen on this trip.

My local Russian business partner, Andrei, picks me up at Arrivals, and during the two-hour taxi ride into Moscow city center, I have a heated conversation with him over the sales results, which are not what I like them to be.

"What do you mean our biggest deal is slipping? You know I have committed this order—we cannot back out now!"

I hear myself raising my voice with all the pent-up stress accumulated on the flight over here. I know I should not be angry at Andrei. The Russian government has stopped funding this particular project, and there is absolutely nothing anybody can do about it. But I clearly need to vent, and I take it out on him.

When I'm done yelling, I feel anxious and uncomfortable. The job has been getting to me lately. The travel has me in a constant state of jet lag. My blood pressure is high, and I have been drinking way too much. I make a feeble attempt to make amends. "Andrei, let's have dinner tomorrow night at that great place on Tverskaya, just off Red Square. Bring your wife. I am buying."

He nods and drops me off at my hotel on Prospect Mira. I can tell that he is boiling inside, but he knows better than to retaliate now, with me in this worked-up state.

I stand for a moment in the freezing cold, watching Moscow traffic, glad to be out of the overheated Lada cab. I try to inhale the crisp, cold air, but I instantly smell gasoline, so I quickly step inside and queue to check into Russia's largest hotel, the two-thousand-room Cosmos. I treasure fond memories of this Soviet-era establishment, where I spent a memorable week with my graduate class of 1988 just before the USSR fell apart.

The look and feel of the place has not changed much over the last twenty years. It is ten PM, and still the hotel lobby is crowded like Grand Central Station, with a confusing mix of Russian businessmen and international tourists. Heineken neon signs flash over the many lobby bars, where stunning Ukrainian girls are still offering their enticing brand of seduction at democratic prices. Another fond memory. The check-in clerk is surly and curt, with a face like a boxer's, affirming my stereotypical memory bias.

While I'm waiting in line, melancholy overwhelms me, and I lose myself in bittersweet retrospection. My mind rewinds back to July 1988. Along with two hundred of my fellow Global Business Majors, I land at Moscow's old Sheremetyevo airport. The mood of the group is elated.

With four years of college under our belt, we are masters in the dynamics of the capitalist free market, and we are intrigued to meet with its exact opposite, the infamous Soviet planned economy. Especially the renowned Moscow black market fascinates me, and I personally plan to test it to its limits.

Guts and glory.

I am wearing a flight bomber jacket just like the one Tom Cruise is sporting in Top Gun, this year's hit movie. I have been advised that I can sell this gear for a great many Soviet Rubles on the streets of Moscow.

And so it happens. That first evening, I don't need to look far for a buyer. People approach me and nervously whisper in subdued voices "I give you Rubles," while tugging at the sleeves of the jacket. After a hurried negotiation, I settle on a significant amount of currency, leveraging the scarcity of Top Gun bomber jackets in a city starved for Western symbols. A seller's market if there ever was one.

With a thick wad of one-hundred-Ruble bills, I proceed to rent the hotel Ball Room for the night, and, with my fellow graduates, I throw a legendary party. We buy a hundred bottles of Sovetskoye Shampanskoye, the Soviet brand of sparkling wine. The stuff is not very good, but it does the job. I am totally in love with Claire, my girlfriend at the time, and the future looks endless and full of possibility. A night not easily forgotten.

At the end of our stay, the Cosmos presents me with a bill for the damaged hotel property. It seemed a great idea on the night of the party to fire our Champagne corks straight up and through the ceiling panels of the Ball Room. I paid that bill willingly, money well spent on a new ceiling, I guess. As they say: "Don't trust a brilliant idea unless it survives the hangover."

Thinking back about that trip behind the Iron Curtain, I can still taste the adrenaline rush of us roaming around an economic wasteland where the normal rules do not apply. It's one of the only times in my life when I felt like a maverick. After that, I lost that free spirit and conformed like the rest of us.

The memory stings, though, because I am now in the exact same place, but I no longer have that sense of excitement and endless possibility. Ironic, because you could call me successful on all counts that mattered to me as a student, and yet I feel only pressure.

Guts and glory, without the glory.

My consciousness returns to the here and now when it is finally my turn at the check-in counter. Without a smile, the clerk says: "Добро пожаловать в космос" (Welcome to the Cosmos). This strikes me as very funny, as if I have just entered another galaxy. The reception clerk, however, does not see the humor in it, and for the next fifteen minutes, he proceeds with inspecting and stamping my passport as if to say: "The USSR came and went, but this is still Russia."

The wear and tear of the journey have me wondering whether it is all worth it, as I wait for the elevator to take me up to the twentieth floor, which houses the Russian version of Executive Suites.

While the elevator is going up, a heavy weight presses me down. As if everything relies on me, while at the same time, I have very little control.

In my room, I am quick to take a Baltika beer from the minibar, and I lay down on the bed with the bottle unopened. I hold the cold glass against my forehead, and I close my eyes.

I want very much to open the bottle, but I hesitate. I already had plenty of wine on the plane over. I am aware that I am using alcohol to calm my nerves, and this has become a steady pattern. I've read it's an addiction when you want to stop and you cannot. What if you do not want to stop?

Well, I am torn and powerless when it comes to alcohol. Nowadays, it is more and more difficult to hold out even until noon for my first drink. I realize this is bad, and panic grips me.

I open the bottle, and I drink.

I tell myself that it's only beer and I'm definitely going to drink less, starting tomorrow. Several beers later, I drift into an uneasy sleep. As if my subconscious cannot wait to tell me something, I am propelled into a dream:

I am fast approaching a tipping point. The tipping point of what, exactly, is not clear. What I know for sure is that, as I come nearer, nothing can be done, and once past it, nothing can be done about it, either. At the same time, I have the strangest sensation that I am not just heading toward the future, but the future is coming toward me with increasing speed. The sensation seems to accelerate until everything suddenly stops and I am in Slow Time. I have never heard of Slow Time, yet somehow I know this is the time that existed before my birth and the time that will continue after my death. I feel very calm as if this is a rite of passage which I have been preparing for all of my life. A sense of well-being covers me like a warm blanket.

I wake up suddenly with a tremendous sense of relief. The hairs on my forearms and neck are standing out, and my heart is beating fast. I have a cathartic sensation of reawakening.

I am alive, and this is my time.

I feel an urgency to capture this essence before it evaporates. Thoughts come in rapid succession. It's in my genes to constantly scenario-plan and to think contingency. What I expect from the future affects my actions in the present and, therefore, impacts the future. I am in a closed loop. I should let go of this illusion of control. Just let things be. Accept loose threads. Embrace imperfection and insecurity.

I breathe slowly and deliberately to calm myself down. I rearrange my thoughts like books on a shelf.

I see a picture in my mind's eye of a mountaintop with a sign stuck in the snow that says: Two PM on Everest.

This was triggered by something I read on the plane over. Top mountaineer Ed Viesturs said: "Getting to the top is optional, getting down is mandatory." He instituted a life-saving rule: "Regardless whether you have reached the top or not, by two PM you turn around to make sure there is enough daylight left on the way down to reach a lower level camp before the evening cold kills you."

It occurs to me that, in every situation, I feel compelled to build in a turnaround point to avoid a point of no return that may or may not be there. It has become a way of life, and it makes me anxious because I know full control is impossible.

The meaning of my dream slaps me in the face. No need for a two PM turnaround point every single day of my life. Why don't I just live a little on the days that I am not climbing Everest?

I look out of my window, high over the roofs of Moscow city. The sun is reflected in the golden onion-shaped domes on the many churches I see. Smoke is circling up in the sky from the many chimneys and is touching the clouds.

It looks like it will snow tonight, as if nature has decided to mercifully cover up the man-made mess down below.

I am tired and lie down on the bed again. I fall into a deep sleep, this time with no dreaming at all, at peace with myself and the cosmos.

CHAPTER 15

RIPPLING

BY CATHERINE LAVORTER

A daline Vikander and I were on a first-name basis now, and we had started to enjoy each other's company. I found her to be bright and cheerful, with sharp insights. Once I had acquired a feel for her abilities as a therapist, I allowed her to participate in the actual patient sessions. And who would have thought that, rather than feeling intimidated by her good looks, most of my patients would actually grow to be more open and talkative with her in the room?

I had not been able, however, to make her change her titillating, secretary-like outfits into something less suggestive, and so I had finally resigned myself to her teasing ensembles. Why she insisted on contrasting her obvious intellect with that particular bimbo look could be the subject matter of a therapy case in itself.

Together, we'd been waiting for Peter in my therapy room for fifteen minutes now. When he finally arrived, he profusely apologized for being late. He wasn't wearing his usual business attire, and I wondered whether he was taking a vacation from work.

Adaline offered him a cup of coffee with a small plate of Sprüngli biscuits, a local delicacy which he accepted with a nod and a weak smile.

Settling down in his usual chair, he said quietly: "Ladies, again my apologies. I hate being late."

"No worries," I said. "How have you been?"

He hesitated for just a moment. I could sense from his body language that something was up. "I am sad to say my father passed away the day before yesterday," he said. "I still feel shell-shocked. The sudden deterioration in his condition took me and my brother and sister completely by surprise. Dad was ninety-four, and I know now that, at that age, things can happen fast. That's what I keep telling myself, but a part of me cannot believe he's gone. A week ago, there were absolutely no signs that this would happen."

I was somewhat taken aback by the fact that he had not called me the day his father died, but I guess he wanted to deliver the news in person during this session.

"I am very sorry to hear that," I responded. "My sincere condolences. How are you coping?"

While I was saying this, Adaline's soft voice chimed in with expressions of sympathy for Peter, and she put her hand on his arm. She definitely went for a more personal approach, and it could not be denied that she did it with a flair all her own.

Peter was clearly moved.

"Thank you both. It's been an emotional week, as you can imagine. I am so glad I had the chance to visit him every day, right up till the end when he lost consciousness, and we had to let him go." He looked heartbroken. "You know, just a month ago, we celebrated his ninety-fourth birthday at my sister's house, where Dad lived since Mom died. The whole family showed up for his birthday; not one person was missing, and I can tell you we have a large family. That in itself is uncanny, like we all knew deep down this was going to be the last time, that there would be no ninety-fifth edition."

He smiled while reminiscing. "On the day of his anniversary, we took this great family picture outside in the garden, with my dad positioned on a chair right in the middle of four generations of his progeny. The younger kids posted the photo on Facebook, and so many people liked it and left comments, it was endearing."

He looked down and concentrated on his shoes for a long minute as if the mystery of life and death would be revealed right there and then. When he looked back up, he said, "That beautiful day with the whole family was the celebration of a lifetime, not just another birthday."

"I am glad you got to have that last memory of him," I said. "You should treasure that."

"Yes. My dad took the photo with him when his condition suddenly got so much worse that we had to rush him to the hospital. He kept looking at the picture like it provided real solace."

"Oh, wow," Adaline said.

"As the days went by, I could feel his consciousness changing," he continued, "like he was getting ready to go home to my mother. Something in him slowly but surely let go of all the worldly stuff. But he held on to that picture as if that was the only thing he wanted to take with him. Maybe, to show to his wife what they had accomplished together on this earth."

He blinked a couple of times. Then he stated in a less emotional voice, as if he felt he had to brace up in the company of two women, "A good way to go, really. I would sign up for an exit like that. I am so glad his doctor administered morphine when it was clear the end was coming; my dad did not suffer much."

"Can it be that what happened with your father has given you the strength to look at death in a new light?" I asked.

He hesitated again. The events of the last week clearly had not given him pause to think about what this meant to him and his anxieties.

"The word that comes to mind is *hope*, Doc."

He sounded inspired.

"Yes, that's it, hope. The dignified way in which my father dealt with his imminent departure gave me hope. It's as if he knew he could give me one last gift by teaching me how to die, modeling how to do it with a level of courage and grace that had seemed utterly impossible until I saw him do it. As if it was just another natural step in his life, rather than something to dread."

He paused and then said in a quiet voice: "It was deeply confrontational and beautiful at the same time."

"Did your dad know about your fear of death?" I probed.

"Well, he knew all about my anxieties, way back when I was young. And I told him a while ago that the old fears had returned after I had stopped drinking. He never gave me advice on how to deal with that, so I had assumed he, too, was at a loss. But I guess he showed me in the end. He showed me good."

"Are you okay if we explore this somewhat deeper? We can do it at a later time if it is too painful now."

"No, that's fine. Talking about it will help me grieve."

"Alright, then. The fact that your dad gave you hope by passing the way he did, could it be that he helped you lift an old taboo, helped you set the record straight on the whole business of death?"

He answered with a question, which is an excellent technique, usually reserved for the therapist in the room. "Did you read my last story? The one in which I dream about the time before I was born and the time after my death?"

"Yes I did. You called it 'Slow Time.' And that dream made you realize that now is your time to be alive and you should savor that."

"When writing that piece, that dream came back to me in a flash," he said. "I had fully repressed it somehow."

"The way you described arriving at the tipping point between past and future—I believe you called it a rite of passage—I thought that was very special. Much like you were returning from a suspended state back to your real self, back to the present you, as it were. There is truth in that. We all need to realize we only have one life and it is only ours to live, now."

"It feels like my life again belongs to me, after a long period of stifling guilt, with the drinking and all the bad stuff I imposed on my family."

I wanted to encourage him about the progress he was making. I could tell that he did not fully realize how far he had come since rehab.

"I strongly believe it is your sobriety which brings about these new insights. I hope you know you are doing good work here; give yourself some credit."

"I do feel a transformation. I feel I want to live again. For the longest time, with my addiction, I just wanted everything to stop."

He turned to glance at Adaline. I could only assume he was unaware that his gaze followed a deliberate path from her eyes down to her legs and back up again. Then he looked back at me.

"That dream also made me realize that what I am really scared about, even more than the actual act of dying, is the thought of not being alive."

"You do realize that you will not experience not being alive?" I said. "Your consciousness will be gone."

"The mere notion of not existing feels unbearable to me. It feels as if all will be truly lost when I am gone. My world, and the significance I have given to all the people and the things in my life, all of that will be gone when I am no longer there to experience it. I hate to think that all I'd tried to do on this earth has been for nothing."

Unexpectedly, Adaline answered, "And then again, your father just demonstrated how to be at the root of a long bloodline and to be remembered and honored for many years to come."

Peter had not seen this coming, this link with his dad's legacy. He took a minute to reflect on this.

"Well, Miss Vikander, you are right. Although my father's gone, in a way he's still here. And not only due to the fact that his genes are carried forward but even more so by what he taught us during a lifetime of caring. My mom and dad were authentic people, and somehow I am still able to tap from that source. Even more so now, that they are no longer here."

"I would like you to capture this feeling in an image, Peter," I said. "Can you try?"

He closed his eyes for a moment. "I get a mental picture of a container slowly being filled to the rim with a precious liquid and then overflowing into a much larger basin. The superabundance is not problematic. The permission to spill over somehow gives meaning to the whole thing. When the container is full, the flow continues, and yet nothing gets spilled, nothing is wasted. Does that make sense?"

I was quietly amused but also glad of the way Adaline had jumped in at the exact right time. With the enthusiasm of the young, she had managed to establish a rapport with Peter which really added value to the session. There definitely was a future in therapy for her.

"Perfect sense," I responded. "You call it 'overflowing'. Dr. Irvin Yalom, a renowned American psychiatrist, calls it 'rippling.'"

"'Rippling'?"

"Yes, like when you throw a rock into a pool of water, it creates ever-widening concentric circles across the surface. This rippling effect, if you will, can take many forms in the context of transcending death."

"How so?"

"When your father set an example of how to go to his end with valor and equanimity, he gave you an antidote for existential fear which you can use on yourself and then in turn pass on to your children. That is a good example of rippling over multiple generations."

"Yes, I get it," he said.

"And also, the fact that your parents' essence will propagate for a long time will bring an element of continuity into the future. Not only their genes but also their values will live on. As you said, the flow will not be interrupted."

"Rippling in ever-widening circles, I like that," he said. "Same principle as paying it forward, right?"

"I had not thought of the parallel, but you could compare the two concepts. Paying it forward is all about doing good, with the aim to inspire and trigger others to do the same. The payoff is not getting something back, but knowing that you propel goodness forward, to keep the cycle going. It has that same rippling effect into the future, on to people whom the initial benefactor might never get to know."

Peter jumped in before I even had fully completed my sentence. "You know, I was recently confronted with an extreme example of that, when I was on a business trip to Singapore. At the time, I did not know you called it 'rippling,' but now I realize that is what it was. The memory of it still shakes me up."

"If you have time, I would love to read about that," Adaline said.

I felt I had to intervene here. "Remember when I introduced Adaline into our sessions a couple of weeks ago, we agreed that I would let her read your stories. Well, I guess she did read the ones you sent to me. I trust that is still okay with you?" I was somewhat apprehensive as I had not expected my dear trainee to come forward like she did, encouraging him to write. I should have told her to refrain from these kind of instructions and leave that to me. But Peter seemed okay with it.

"Well, although I do feel a bit self-conscious about those stories, I guess I'm fine with it, for the sake of progress. We did agree that Miss Vikander could read them, so I should not be surprised."

"I feel like your stories tell me even more about you than the sessions," Adaline said. "Or better, they are oddly complementary. Together, they are more than just the sum of the separate parts."

Peter seemed flattered hearing her say this. "Alright, I will try to put my recent Singapore experience into words. The incident has left a deep impression on me, and I want to put that to good use."

I looked at the clock and tried to get us back on track. "In the time we have left for today, I would like to briefly touch again upon your preoccupation with control."

Peter nodded.

"In your last story, 'Tipping Point,' you rightly conclude that you really should let go of the constant contingency planning, when there is no real need. You made a great analogy with the two PM turnaround rule in mountaineering. You said that on the days you're not climbing Everest, you should relax and let go. Did that insight have any lasting effect on you?"

"Writing that indeed made me realize that I should not worry about the future all the time and just accept the facts as they are now. But insight is one thing, Doc; turning that into actual change is quite another. I seem to be unable to stop myself from looking for certainty and security." He sighed. "At least, I understand better now that this is an area I need to work on. That's a start."

"Do you know the expression, *If you want to make God laugh, tell him about your plans*?" Adaline asked. "To me, that really says it all. Control over what will happen tomorrow is an illusion. We should focus on today and let the rest unfold."

Making a mental note to come back to this in the next session, I said, "Things will never go the way your mind wants them to. Insisting all the time on getting everything just right according to your personal preferences just causes frustration. You expect your mind to fix the world for you. But as you know by now, that will not happen. Give it a rest."

CHAPTER 16

ETHER

BY PETER BAER

My taxi got stuck in the evening traffic on Singapore's Orchard Road so I gave the cabbie a solid tip and proceeded on foot. Slightly out of breath, I walked up the stairs of the Raffles Hotel and into its famous Long Bar. My friend Arthur was sitting with a cold Tiger Beer in hand and talking animatedly into his phone.

I sat down and ordered a Singapore Sling, which, by the way, was first created in this very bar in 1915. I grinned at Arthur, who gesticulated that he was trying to finish up his call. I looked around and took in the wonderful ambiance of the place.

Named after the founder of Modern Singapore, Sir Stamford Raffles, and immortalized in the novels of

Rudyard Kipling and Somerset Maugham, the Raffles Hotel just breathes heritage. The elegant stateliness of the old mansion, with its British Colonial-style furnishings, makes it more legend than hotel.

We sat on low rattan sofas on dark hardwood flooring, and, from the high ceiling, authentic Diehl fans produced a soft humming noise while their blades cut through the air. The walls were filled with displays of globes and telescopes. We looked out through shuttered French windows onto a wide veranda with teak lounge chairs. The sound of crickets chirping in the cool night outside made the tropical mood complete.

Arthur is a large, bald man, and as usual, he was dressed like he just came back from a week in the outback. He moved to Singapore a year ago with his wife and three children after a four-year stint in the moist heat of Chennai, India. Addicted to expat life, the couple has sworn never to return to their roots in cold, wet Europe.

Arthur and I go back a long way and feel at ease with each other, without the need for a lot of words.

Our plan for the evening was to head out to the Esplanade music theatre in Marina Bay near the mouth of the Singapore River, where Australian rock band Tame Impala were scheduled to do a live gig tonight. On an impulse, I had bought the tickets online that morning at twice the face value because Arthur and I both love the band's psychedelic sound, which blends rock with dreamy melodies.

The band's off-the-wall personality is reflected in their name, which refers to an impala, an African antelope known for its typical nervousness and capable of jumping up to three meters in the air when startled. Tame Impala then points to the one, un-vexed specimen grazing the savanna, which lets you come closer and make real contact. Pretty cool name for a crew of talented musicians who project a maturity beyond their young age.

As if brought on by my thinking, I heard a TV voice saying: "Although very weak, she will attend tonight's performance of Tame Impala by special invitation of the band." My interest triggered, I looked up at the large LCD screen above the bar and recognized the portrait of Michelle, the young girl who recently became the nation's symbol of suffering and hope. Everyone knows her as the sweet seventeen-year-old who has been on the waiting list for a heart transplant for four months now. The entire population of South-East Asia has been following her story ever since she collapsed on stage, on national television. That fateful evening, Michelle was performing a violin solo as the Singapore nominee for the widely popular Asian Youth Orchestra competition for best classical performer under eighteen.

When she'd entered the stage, she walked with confidence, head up high. Her long, black hair framed her delicate face, and she radiated the sophistication that came with a privileged and classical upbringing. The image of the elegant young soloist in black evening dress giving her very best to Paganini's "Caprice No. 4" and then suddenly passing out on the podium has, since that dramatic event, been burned in the collective memory of millions of viewers.

When it'd happened, it had taken a long twenty seconds before the entire orchestra finally stopped playing, and then there was nothing but an eerie silence. A general awareness took hold of the audience that this was not just the harmless fainting of a young woman under the glaring heat of spotlights. A few drops of blood had dripped from her nostrils and a TV camera had zoomed in before the editor decided this was too intrusive. The camera moved away quickly to take on a more discreet angle, but the close-up of the blood on the wooden floor remained fixated on the audience's retinas.

The seriousness of her condition was soon confirmed by a doctor in the audience who established heart failure as a diagnosis and gestured that emergency transportation was needed. The audience held its breath, fearful of losing a talented young soul, representing the best of the nation.

TV stations continued their live broadcasting while Michelle was evacuated by helicopter to the Singapore National Heart Centre, with ever more viewers tuning in throughout Asia as the word spread. Several international news crews, including *CNN* and *CNBC*, who had been covering Singapore's parliamentary elections, switched focus and followed in her wake. They set up camp right across the hospital's front entrance and made sure also the Western world became aware of Michelle's affliction.

Once the cardio team had stabilized her, it emerged that Michelle's coronary artery was so dangerously narrowed that her heart function had dipped to just twelve percent and her blood pressure had sunk to a near-lethal level. It was nothing short of a miracle that she had not fallen into a coma when she'd lost consciousness on stage. The hospital hooked her up to the heart-lung machine, which immediately started pumping blood round her body.

That had been four months ago. Michelle had regained consciousness a week or so after the collapse but had remained very fragile ever since.

From day one, she had been on the transplant list with top priority status A1, reserved for the critically ill. Any matching donor heart is offered first to a patient with that designation, but while in the US and Europe the average waiting time is four months, in Singapore it is double that. Too few donor hearts are available on the island city-state, and, as a consequence, more than forty percent of patients do not survive the wait for a heart. This cruel statistic has been quoted in the news almost on a daily basis since Michelle's breakdown and has triggered wide public indignation.

Obtaining a healthy matching heart for Michelle had proven impossible so far. On three occasions the South-East Asia Transplant Network came close. The first potential donor tested positive for cocaine, however, and the second showed signs of hepatitis C. The most recent donor case had raised hopes, but close investigation of the living cadaver showed the victim had not only suffered a head injury but also a chest trauma with evidence of cardiac damage, so again a no-go.

That was three weeks ago.

Since then each day came and went without donor news, and Michelle's condition deteriorated to a point at which her physician told the public to hope for the best but expect the worst. He stated his patient had only the smallest possible window for survival with a life expectancy of less than a week without a transplant.

The image on TV now switched to Tame Impala's lead singer, who explained in Aussie-speak that the band came to know that Michelle liked their music, and they had invited her to attend that night's concert if her condition would allow. He had spoken to Michelle on the phone two days ago, and she had confirmed she would love to be there.

Then Michelle's cardiologist came on screen and stated that his patient's condition was rated as extremely severe and only a last-minute donor heart could mean the difference between life and death. Yet, there were no signs that a match could be found in the coming hours. Therefore, he would respect Michelle's wish to be present at the concert that evening, and he would be there right at her side.

The specialist spoke in a matter-of-fact tone, as if this kind of thing occurred on a daily basis. And it probably did with many patients who were not in the public eye and had to suffer their fate in silence. In any case, his words sent shivers down my spine.

I looked around me in the Raffles' Long Bar, and absolutely everybody was sitting motionless, with their eyes fixated on the screen. Clearly, my peers here were also deeply affected by the events unfolding, and we felt strangely connected by this harsh confrontation with the fragility of life.

It was very hard to believe that science or money could not save the life of this precious young girl. Even that very morning, the CEO of Singapore Telecom had pledged their corporate jet to fly in a healthy heart from anywhere within a six-hour radius, which was the maximum time a donor heart would remain viable. But without a last-minute match, that plane would stay where it was, on the tarmac of Changi International Airport. It felt as if a higher force wanted to show who ultimately had the power.

When the news anchor finally changed topics, Arthur and I discussed what to do next. We both had mixed feelings about tonight. We wanted to go to the concert because we had tickets to see one of our favorite bands play live. But the last thing we wanted was to be voyeurs, selected by fate to witness up close the very delicate situation of this young girl on the verge of dying. We both wanted to do the respectful thing, but it was hard to figure out what that was.

In the end, we decided we would go to the concert because we wanted to be united with other people wishing that this would end well. Maybe the massive public support would give Michelle the strength to hang on another day.

The event hall, nicknamed the Durian, as the twin structures with the thousands of spiky protuberances resemble the pungent national fruit of Singapore, was already filled to the brim when we arrived. We wrestled our way through the crowd to our designated places right in the middle of the arena. We watched in silence as up front, near the podium, an area was cleared by security and a medical team took their places.

Michelle was brought in on a special bed, hooked up to an intimidating amount of medical equipment, just five minutes before the concert started. Her face was projected briefly on two huge screens. She looked incredibly frail and vulnerable, yet somehow she managed a faint smile and waved briefly at the camera as if she wanted to say "Thanks" for having her here.

A surge of emotion went through the audience, and her name started reverberating through the large hall. Not loud but rather like a thousand whispers converging into one, as if the joint human presence here knew exactly how to pay tribute to this sacred moment and this brave girl, hanging on to life.

Tame Impala opened with a subdued statement: "Good evening, Singapore, and a special welcome to Michelle. We in the band hope you will enjoy this concert tonight."

The two large screens projected only the stage, where the band performed the first three songs of their set. Gradually the crowd eased into the evening and seemed to forget about the special guest. Then suddenly the musicians stopped playing, and the lead singer gently made the crowd go quiet and said, facing the hospital bed: "Michelle, you told us that 'Let It Happen' is your favorite song, and we want to dedicate it to you tonight".

It took a moment for the crowd to take this in.

The lyrics of the band's signature song, "Let It Happen," and its typical, effervescent sound make it a spiritual, almost hallucinatory piece. Its meaning centers on accepting a personal transition in a world of chaos: It does not help to resist; it takes more energy to shut it all out than it does to let it happen.

In any normal, non-life-or-death situation, that wisdom makes perfect sense. But projected onto Michelle's predicament, this triggered a deep concern in everybody present. What exactly was the message here? "Let it happen," as in "Do not resist, and surrender to dying"? Surely, this is not what the band meant. This whole thing was either completely inappropriate or exactly right.

A murmur went through the crowd as people speculated whether Michelle indeed wanted to give them a sign here tonight. Or was this song just the personal favorite of a teenager enjoying a rare and special night out?

The song started, and soon the crowd was overwhelmed by a massive wall of synth sound, filling the music hall with an exceptional cosmic ambiance and magical vocoder harmonies. The screens now projected the face of Michelle, who seemed to be crying softly with her eyes closed. She apparently experienced difficulty breathing, which was painful to watch. But then, near the end of the song, she opened her eyes, and her face lit up. She smiled softly, and she seemed to radiate a sense of peace.

Whenever groups of people together experience a challenging situation and reach a higher emotional state, their collective awareness starts resonating at a higher frequency range. Upon seeing Michelle smile, exactly such a vibration of increased consciousness rippled through the crowd.

People were confused and upset but mostly just hopeful. They wanted so much to be reassured that this was a good thing, that Michelle was feeling the love, and that there was still time and a way to save her.

Surely she would not just vaporize like ether into the open air, although there was no denying it felt like that could happen here tonight. It was a tender moment, and we all knew it.

Suddenly, the doctor next to her bed took Michelle's pulse and shined a light into her pupils. He then gave urgent instructions to his medical team, and the bed was rushed out of sight. A couple of minutes later, we heard a helicopter taking off, and then the two screens showed it speeding away. The audience was in disarray. The cameras switched back to the band's lead singer who spoke in a soft voice: "Ladies and gentlemen, we will pray for Michelle the only way we know how to."

With that, an acoustic version of "The Moment" washed over the audience, and people just stood there, until the song was over. I think each of us prayed to his or her personal God, even those who did not at all believe. Especially those. Arthur and I walked home in silence. We communicated without words, as old friends do.

Early the next morning, I boarded the first river-boat taking off from Clarke Quay, where Singapore River starts to cut through the heart of the city. A hot wind blew in my face while I took deep breaths of clean morning air and felt alive. I also felt privi-leged and somehow enlightened by the events of the evening before. I mostly wanted to be alone on the water to contemplate the meaning of what happened after Michelle was evacuated from the Esplanade concert theater.

Michelle did pass away during the helicopter transfer to the hospital. Her weak heart finally gave up in mid-air. There was absolutely nothing the doctors could do. And after her family had said their goodbyes, Michelle's vital organs were harvested because she carried a donor card.

Social media this morning showcased last night's Tame Impala concert and Michelle's presence there as a special guest. "Her Last Public Appearance" was the headline on the front page of *The Straits Times*. But most of all, they were all over the fact that five people during the night had gotten a new lease on life, one of them a seven-year-old Australian girl who played the violin and received one of Michelle's lungs. Yes, Michelle did let it happen last night, but she did it on her own terms. She made sure the world got to know her, and that knowing would now ripple onwards.

CHAPTER 17

LOCKED IN THE BASEMENT

BY CATHERINE LAVORTER

"That sure was one gripping account of what 'rippling' means, Peter." I had already started talking while Peter was still settling in, but he seemed utterly distracted and did not respond. He was fumbling his cell phone out of his pocket and put it on vibrate.

"I loved how Michelle's unmistakable radiance transcended her own death. Her essence rippled through the entire nation and seemed to fill a void. The comparison with ether expanding into a vacuum was spot on."

Adaline Vikander had been waiting impatiently for me to finish. "Man, rippling does not get any more real than that," she said. "It must have given Michelle tremendous strength to know that others would live on thanks to her organs. Speaking of purpose." She used her beaming smile at Peter and added, "Poignant story, Peter, right on the mark."

Peter just nodded and looked forlorn. But Adaline had no intention of letting it go just yet. She had told me before the session that she had been intrigued by his detached style.

"If I may. You write Michelle's narrative in a very reserved manner, but at the same time, you seem deeply touched. Why use this restraint in the writing?" She waited for a reaction, but none was forthcoming, so she continued. "You formulate your sentences with surgical precision. I can almost smell the disinfectant, so to speak. Are you aware you seem to decontaminate your stories before you bring them out into the open?"

No answer. She was now quickly coming to the end of her patience. She let out a deep sigh while speaking. "Peter, what I'm trying to get at is this. You only allow yourself to be a reporter of the events really, while you're obviously eager to participate and to feel what there is to feel. Could it be that you're threatened by the emotions brought on by your own writing and that you keep yourself in lockdown?"

Again he remained silent, and now I really wondered what was going on. From Adaline's frustrated expression, I could see that she did not appreciate the way he was treating her. I understood her reaction, but on the other hand, she still had ways to learn that therapy is to the benefit of the patient and not always a mutual exercise of intellectual gratification.

Then Peter spoke out as if a thick fog had suddenly lifted from his brain. "I apologize, ladies, but I am sick and tired of feeling the way I do. I feel like shit!" He gave us an agonized look. "I've been sitting here, trying to find a way to describe the awful state I'm in, but I cannot find the words. Best I can come up with is 'anxious badness?'"

Adaline and I looked at him and then at each other, with what must have been big question marks on our faces. He saw that more information was required. "Look, I'm hurting here, and I need your help to bring to the surface whatever is causing it. It drives me crazy that this pain is always there, just beyond my grasp. I want to reach down to the bottom of the pit and let the black despair come up. I am ready to cut and drain the abscess." He ran both hands through his hair and then looked at us both, relieved, it seemed, that the words had finally come out.

I felt inadequate that I had not picked up on his bottled-up tension when he had first entered my office. How could I have missed that? The important thing now was that he was ready to deal with his unresolved anxiety.

"What strikes me," I said, "is that you often switch between being this controlling person, driven by pure logic, and then being fair game for your repressed emotions, which spiral up in the moment and completely overwhelm you. Is the latter an accurate description of what is happening here today?"

"Yes, Doc, this is very real to me. These undercurrents take me away."

"You called it 'anxious badness.' Are you aware that's a fair definition of guilt?"

"Guilt?" He looked surprised and intrigued at the same time.

"I take it that with 'badness,' you mean 'evil,' right? Maybe we could even call it 'sin,' given the sensitivity for all things religion which you developed when you were a boy?

"Yes, it feels like a voice inside is constantly judging and blaming me. Absolution seems forever out of reach, to put it in the Catholic context."

"Let me tell you about your guilt and fears, Peter. They represent the basement level in the house of human consciousness, and you are still locked in there. You want to find the key and get the hell out of there. Run up the stairs to a higher level, where the perspective on life is much better." I wanted to make it absolutely clear to him that he is a free agent when it comes to his anxieties, not just a victim. He has the power to do something about them. "Whenever you're dwelling down there, in those low, egotistic states, your energies are drained by a constant struggle for emotional survival. You are not advancing because you are bogged down by your baser emotions. That is what I see happening here. "

"That may well be, but I don't know what to do about that." He was on the defensive now.

"You call them 'undercurrents,' and rightly so. It is very true that you cannot control these inferior feelings—they control you. There is no space for anything else down there. That state feels utterly compulsive, and it can drive you to despair when you linger too long." I now had his full attention. He looked at me with a mix of hope and anguish. "But then again, that very suffering has the power to make you want to break free of it."

"How so?"

"Anxiety has a function. It's an essential reminder of your aliveness and a normal part of the recovery process."

"Do you mean that my fears are actually pushing me upwards?" he asked.

"Ever since you stopped drinking, you have been fighting your way up to a more positive mental state. Your frustration about the unresolved guilt and fears is what makes you feel like shit. You are locked in that basement, while you know there's a number of floors above your head."

Rather than seeing this argument through to its logical conclusion, he switched gears. "You talk about guilt. But what do I have to be guilty about? I am fighting like hell to stay sober. I am working day in, day out to provide for my family, to be a good husband and father. But the more I try to make amends for what I have done wrong during my drinking years, the further away atonement seems to be. That drives me fucking crazy."

"Those feelings of remorse are for sure not caused by anything you do or not do in the present," I responded. "As you know, you are doing very well in terms of recovery, and I admire how you travel the world and still stay on top of things at home." I could tell this brought him some relief, but it would be short-lived if I could not substantiate my point. "The self-accusations are just negative programming from your past. They are old recordings that your ego keeps replaying, with the outside world as a punishing bad parent and you as a helpless and hopeless victim."

"Old recordings."

"Yes, that is correct. It is time now to throw those tapes away because they are archaic and irrelevant." I wanted him to understand that well-being is a decision. It does not just happen; he needs to make it happen. "Now that you have made the commitment to stay sober, you have come to realize that you can aim for real happiness. It is not your destiny to simply grin and bear the pain of your negative emotions. Real freedom in the psychological and spiritual sense is within your reach. Adaline earlier today said that you seem to be on lockdown, in protective mode, and she was right. Now is the time to open up."

He nodded slowly. "So it is up to me, is it?"

"Yes. It is up to you, but you have to remove some roadblocks to get there. You've got a taste of what it means to feel good again, and this now triggers anger in you because you want to get rid of the albatross around your neck, but you do not know how."

"So this guilt I feel is nothing but a reflex from the past?"

"Yes, a critical voice in you still finds fault with even your most basic human drives. I can see that the mere mention of the words 'sin' and 'guilt' bring back instant repulsion. You feel you deserve to leave all this excess baggage behind, yet it still has the power to cut you down to size. Am I right?"

His face showed that we were on the same page. "I am breaking my head over this, Doc. I really have no clue how to cut loose this deadweight."

"And as always, you're using your rational mind to intellectualize your pain away. You even use the expression *break your head*, which is rather funny. By agonizing over this, you suppress rather than face your grief."

"I think too much. I know. So what now?"

"You should bypass the mind and try to go one level higher, one which is now clearly within your reach."

"Which level is that?"

"Courage."

"Come again?"

"Courage and anxiety are two flipsides to the same coin. With a dose of courage, you can bite the bullet and face the fears you have subdued for so long. You can decide to dare them until they no longer have a stronghold over you."

"So I make a stand and defy my fears?"

"Yes. Stare them down. Confront your terrors head-on, and stare them down. Then move on, leave that basement, and do not look back. Expand your view of the world, and enjoy new experiences. You will see that the anxiety will run out of energy and dissipate." I could read from his desolate expression that he found the prospect of a direct confrontation with his fears a precarious proposition. All his earlier talk about draining the abscess was clearly hard to put into practice.

"Peter, I am not being flippant here. Even if this feels like a very risky path, you should nevertheless take it."

He nodded slowly.

"Remember our Mount Everest analogy? This is your window to ascend further to the top, because the sun has just come out from behind the clouds. You have a narrow but clear corridor to the summit. Just find the audacity to pack up your gear and get going!"

"Okay—let's see if I get this right. So you're saying that by moving forward in a single-minded way, by recovering the gutsiness from my younger days, my fears will eventually lose their powers?"

"Yes! Trust me, this is a track you will want to follow all the way to the end. And that end could be happiness or at least peace of mind. Whatever happens, try to reach the upper floors in your house of consciousness. The view is so much better from up there."

"How do you know that I even have access to this kind of courage?" he asked.

"Not to worry, Peter, the courage is there. We would not be talking about this if deep inside, you would not want to overcome your fears. But until now, you did not seem to realize this was up to you. You did not see it even as an option. What I am doing today, is to empower you."

He liked that. "I want so much to believe you. All I want is to be on the move again, with a new sense of possibility."

"Yes, and one more thing. I encourage you to give room to the intuition that there is something inside you that you no longer expected to find."

"What's that?"

"You are in the process of rediscovering your natural self, the part of you that you loved so much when you were a boy. I refer to that capacity in you to explore the world with open eyes, without the constantly disapproving voice playing in the background."

"You mean the child version of me is still in there?"

"Yes, that part of you has always been there, but it got corrupted by the alpha male ego, the killer job, the frantic lifestyle, and, of course, the drinking."

This clearly resonated. Peter had an earnest look on his face as he took the words in. He kept his silence for a full minute, deep in thought. Then he took the bait. "Well, lately I've felt this new emotion. It's hard to describe, but it's like coming home after a long, hard journey. Coming home to myself, it feels like. It's as if I'd forgotten all this time that there is more to me than my problems and my constant preoccupation with status and money. It's indeed like I'm rediscovering the boy in me."

"Tell me more—what's it like?" I asked.

"Thinking out loud here. Words that come to mind are: *Unspoiled, guilt-free, unadulterated.* It feels like innocence recaptured. These bright flashes of purity have been few and far between, but they're undeniably there."

"Can you tell me exactly what triggers these mental blue skies? Thoughts and emotions are like the weather: The sun is always there behind the clouds—sometimes you see it, and sometimes you don't."

He did not have to think long. "Well, at times I hear a sound that moves me, and suddenly everything is okay. I am okay. I never experienced that in all the years while I was drinking, but now I do. Like I did when I was a young boy."

I was very glad to hear this. It was not often that Peter would admit to the glass being half-full. Of course, he was quick to qualify it further.

"Not just any sound, mind you, but certain tone colors seem to bring me back to a preverbal time in my life before words and concepts existed, a time when everything was sound, pure and simple."

I waited for more to bubble up.

"Sometimes when I am driving in my car, and I'm listening to a female voice on the radio, I get carried way back in time. A space and silence gets created in me that brings back the small boy inside."

I was about to ask why a female voice, but obviously there was a link to his mother here. It also triggered more questions in me about his strong susceptibility to the allure of women in general, apart from the obvious sexual ones.

He continued. "Likewise, there are times when I am high up in the mountains, and the view feels celestial. Or when I am simply blown away by the beauty of a girl."

"What happens on these occasions?" I asked.

"My mind seems to come to a complete stop, and that absolute stillness is the gateway to something out of this world. In these divine moments, I wish I could believe in God." He was staring at his shoes again. He looked up when I spoke.

"You are describing the sensation of experiencing your real inner self. When the mind stops its incessant play of thoughts and emotions, when the ego falls away, when time seems to stand still, we get a glimpse of what we really are in our core."

"Real heavy stuff, but I'm happy we had this discussion," he said. "My biggest hurdle is the old self-condemnation, though. If I could only get rid of that anxious feeling of badness which I mentioned earlier."

"I believe you have a high propensity toward existential guilt. I think you feel you have disappointed the little boy in you who believed so hard in his own potential in his wonder years. You feel guilty because you did not enter the door that he held open for you. Instead, you opened another one, one that little Peter did not care for."

"Damn, I think you might be right. I feel like I have betrayed myself, there and then."

"Indeed. In the eyes of little Peter, you strayed; you did not stay true to character. I think you regret that now; you wish you could have stayed more authentic."

He nodded.

"Life threw you a number of ambitious challenges, and you've accepted those instead. You rushed to settle for the first social role and matching personality that came within reach, that of the all-important businessman."

"But I always thought that was my purpose in life," he said, "to be successful and provide for my family. That is what my dad expected from me."

"Yes, but you became set in your ways and stuck into that grandiose, overbearing persona. You spent your life in bad faith, acting as if being an omnipotent manager is in fact your essence. Which it clearly is not."

"A hard thing to come to grips with."

"I understand that, but better face up to it now. Why don't you try your hand at a story about this guilt you have felt all this time for not living up to your true potential?"

He thought for a moment. "You know, I think I know just what to write. Something bad happened in Bangkok when I was still drinking. Possibly the worst thing I did in my life. I never told anyone. Maybe now is the time to come clean."

"Sure. Give it a try." I wondered what he meant. I hope he was not going to confess to murder or anything like that. "Put all of this now in the right perspective, and try to forgive yourself. Absolve yourself from the guilt of being you."

CHAPTER 18

HUBRIS

BY PETER BAER

With one eye closed, I look at the clock in my hotel room, and I observe that it's past ten AM A splitting headache defines my being.

I get dressed slowly and painfully and decide to go up to the Octave Rooftop Bar on the forty-seventh floor of the Bangkok Marriott, where I'm staying. The sky lounge on the roof of the hotel offers a fabulous 360-degree view of downtown Bangkok.

The bright-blue luminous cocktail bar is open, but I am the only customer at this early hour. The bartender welcomes me in a cheerful way and picks up instantly on my apparent need for restorative liquid medicine.

"Josephine" by London band Ritual is playing through the bar's sound system, and the melancholic tune sets the proper scene for me to nurse my hangover. The song's elegant, understated sound is the perfect backdrop to the noise and pollution inside my head and below on the streets.

The bartender puts a Siam Mary in front of me, Bangkok's version of the stalwart Bloody Mary. It's one hell of a fiery drink, and I'm sure it will jolt my system into functioning again. This Thai version of the morning-after cocktail surprises with a red-hot twist of Thai chili, lemon, and coriander, blended with the usual suspects vodka, tomato juice, Tabasco and Worcestershire sauce.

This mixture will have to double as my breakfast and a potent fix. While I'm stirring my cocktail, I marvel at the city's skyline which presents itself as absolutely golden under a glorious morning sun.

Bangkok's local name is Krung Thep, or City of Angels. It's where the immortal divinity dwells and the reincarnated angels reside, according to local religious teachings. For the true believers, I'm sure that, from this spot, you could reach up and touch the heavens if you wanted to. A gateway if there ever was one.

I try to get a grip on what exactly occurred last night. What I know for sure is that I took a group of customers out for a night on the town, but I have a hard time remembering the sequence of events. From two AM onwards, it's all a blur. I know for sure that we started out for cocktails at The Glaz Bar on the Plaza

Athenee, a great place to chill and listen to the smooth sounds of brilliant jazz. Bang in the middle of Bangkok, there's no better venue than The Glaz Bar to start the evening. But then the customer suggested we might go to a gentlemen's club after dinner, and someone suggested The Pimp, a very upscale nightclub, famous for its Coyotes.

Coyotes are part and parcel of the upmarket Thai nightlife scene. Drop-dead gorgeous girls whose main task is to entertain businessmen with sensual dancing and to be their hostesses for the evening. The ladies are far classier than the girls in the notorious go-go bars around the city. While Coyotes are officially unavailable for anything but strictly dancing, unofficially, of course, anything is possible. A mere drink with a Coyote costs a fortune; that much I've learned.

Our group arrived at The Pimp just after midnight. A line-up of supercars was parked ostentatiously in front of the red-carpeted club entrance. Looking at the 1966 Red Corvette Convertible, the Shelby Mustang 350, and the golden Maserati parked side by side, I remember I got slightly uncomfortable, worrying how exactly I was going to justify the expense of this gentlemen's club to the company.

Once we got passed the towering doorman by means of a hefty tip, we entered a swanky space with deluxe sofas and armchairs scattered around a central stage. We were met by the lady of the house and led to the perfect spot that could accommodate our party of six. Immediately, we were accompanied by a matching number of hostesses, and, out of nowhere, the booze started flowing.

The Coyotes assigned to us worked hard the next couple of hours to create a fun, erotic atmosphere by dancing and playing drinking games. Sweetly seductive within clearly defined house rules, they were drilled to keep our champagne flutes filled at all times. One girl, who was clearly our Purser for the evening, kept asking me every half hour whether it was okay to order another magnum bottle of Veuve Clicquot. By then, I had very few inhibitions left, so I kept saying "Yes."

As milestones go, I remember us moving from magnum to jeroboam-sized bottles, but after that point, I only have flashes and hazy images. I seem to recall watching my customer dance wildly on the bar, joined by two of the girls and shouting to me this was the best evening ever. That seemed OK with me, at the time. I remember thinking to myself that it was important to keep the customer happy, and I was obviously doing an excellent job at that.

But now I find myself here, on the roof of my hotel, trying to reconstruct how the hell the evening ended. On top of my killer hangover, my conscience is giving me a hard time because not only do I not remember when I left the party or how I got back to the Marriott, I also do not recall saying goodbye to my customer, let alone making sure they got back home safely.

I decide to face the music, and I take out the bill from the gentlemen's club, which I seem to have folded neatly into my wallet. I blink a couple of times before I can focus on the total charge of one hundred thousand Thai Baht, which equals a whopping two thousand eight hundred US dollars. How the hell could the check have worked out magically to an exact number like one hundred thousand Baht?

I am staring at my very own signature at the bottom of the bill, and I wonder what possessed me to sign this. No doubt Miss Purser convinced me at the end of the evening to round off to the nearest hundred. In this case that would have been the nearest one hundred thousand Baht. She'd done a professional con job on me; you had to admire her skills of persuasion.

I am keenly aware of the fact that my company has zero tolerance when it comes to misinterpretation of expenses. The check from The Glaz Bar could justifiably be described as customer entertainment, but a bar bill of a couple of thousand dollars from a gentlemen's club called The Pimp would undoubtedly be seen as abuse and would trigger an awkward conversation between an HR representative and myself.

Well, what's done is done, so I decide to let it rest for now; I would have to deal with it later. I take a deep breath of crisp morning air and then quickly finish my Bloody Mary. For a moment, I hesitate, but then I decide against a second one, as I want to get moving on my day. I need to go and see another customer across town. My head is still pounding, and I have trouble focusing, but this is a common state lately.

Riding the elevator down from the rooftop lounge, I am confronted with a Russian glam couple in the process of seriously making out. For sure not holding back on my behalf, their hands are all over each other. He's in a black Armani shirt and trousers with handcrafted Italian shoes, no socks. She's in sky-high heels, a glittery miniskirt, and a short white fur coat. She's a natural Ural beauty with light eyes, blond hair, and impeccable makeup. She looks twenty-one, but I would not be surprised if she was seventeen, if that.

While he holds one hand under her skirt, she smiles at me with a nerve that throws me off balance. Watching my apparent discomfort, she whispers in her boyfriend's ear, "Пусть смотреть" (Let him watch). He laughs and says, "Вы высмеивать" (You're a tease).

I have a basic understanding of Russian, so I have the hardest time not blushing. This must be their grand finale to a hot night out in Bangkok. Forbidden sex in an elevator riding up to the highest rooftop bar in the city. A total stranger watching their public indecency only adds to the excitement.

While descending the forty-seven floors, I notice that lover boy has been holding her panties folded in his hand all this time. The girl gives me a defiant look, one that says she knows I know. I can't help myself but feel embarrassed and aroused in equal measures.

While stepping out, I notice the closed circuit TV cameras in the lift, and it occurs to me that Thailand has ridiculously strict indecent-exposure laws. I am sure the couple has been equally aware of the CCTV and that very fact just enhanced their experience. Russians are known not to give a damn, and that stereotype just got reconfirmed. Relieved, I get out on the ground floor while they stay in the elevator doing their thing.

Recomposing myself, I check my briefcase and ask reception to quickly call a cab to take me to my customer meeting. I switch to business mode, and, instantly, I feel in control. Back on familiar territory, I feel a lot better. I am the sheriff in this town. I can do this with my eyes closed.

Or with a hangover, for that matter. There is not an obstacle I cannot find my way around when I am focused on the job.

My hotel is located in Thonglor, the trendiest neighborhood of sprawling Bangkok. My customer's offices are on the other side of the city, though, so I tell my taxi driver to hurry up because I'm already late.

Last night, before meeting my customer, I strolled out of the hotel to explore the many art galleries and funky boutiques of local Thai designers. But here and now in this worn-out taxi cab, I see only busy streets and traffic jams prohibiting me from reaching my destination.

I have a lingering sense that something is fundamentally wrong, but I cannot put my finger on it. I tap my driver on the shoulder and urge him to get a move on. I am aware I'm still in the frenzy of intoxication. The alcohol in my blood makes me act out the role of hard-driving, cold-hearted executive. But all this grandiosity, this self-glorification cannot prevent me from feeling more vulnerable than ever in my life. Why do I feel it can all come crashing down any time now?

God, I need to break this ruminative cycle before I go crazy. To distract me, I look outside at the locals weaving through traffic on their scooters and the unavoidable tourists in tuk-tuks. Originating from an old-fashioned rickshaw during the Second World War, a tuk-tuk is essentially the same but with a small engine fitted in. A tourist trap, and a dangerous one at that.

I look at the Raymond Weil watch on my wrist that my wife got me for my birthday last month in Geneva, and it tells me with Swiss precision that indeed I am going to be late. This is unnerving because it means a bad start to the meeting. My customer, a man of tradition and appreciative of old-fashioned punctuality, will see this as a sign of disrespect. Damn. I put my hand on the driver's shoulder again and tell him in a stern voice to find a faster route.

The guy flinches. This whole situation seems to make him extremely jumpy. He's probably used to driving tourists at a leisurely pace through this great city, and now he's here, taking this unforgiving guy in a suit all the way to Silom, Bangkok's financial district. The cabbie keeps mumbling something incomprehensible, clearly upset. But I do not pick up on his distress signals. Rather, I'm cursing myself for not having taken the Skytrain, the elevated rapid transit system recommended strongly by the hotel.

Bad decision, but too late now. We're on Sukhumvit Street, the main traffic artery to the financial district. There is no shortcut. I will just have to sweat it out and apologize to the customer for my lateness.

My driver looks frantically to the left, then to the right, then left again. I see he's soaked with sweat, which is unusual for a local. I suddenly notice with a shock now how his pupils are dilated, betraying mental turmoil. I feel an urgent need to get the hell out of this vehicle.

But before I can say anything, the cabbie makes a wild turn to the left into an insanely narrow street. He accelerates to sixty miles per hour, and we reach the main crossroads at this really crazy speed without slowing down. I'm opening my mouth to tell him to watch out when I see her.

The little girl on the bike. The little girl in the red dress.

The image of the fiery red dress right in front of the car is instantly burned into my eyes. I cannot make a sound. I think I'm pointing my finger at the girl, but I cannot be sure. In my peripheral vision, I see the face of the driver now expressing pure horror, knowing that bad karma is upon him.

My heart skips a beat and then another. My mouth feels ultra-dry, I do not have enough saliva to swallow. I actually see the hair on my arms stand out while I keep gripping the front seat with my both hands as if I could stop the car that way.

In this one instant before impact, I see things with absolute clarity. It all makes dreadful sense. I've been on the wrong track. And this is what it has led to.

Exactly. What. I. Deserve.

The driver, now on auto-pilot and pure adrenaline, tries a desperate maneuver to avoid the girl. Defying gravity, he succeeds in swerving just an inch so he does not hit the child's body but only the rear of her bike. The brutal collision catapults the child away with a velocity that I am sure will kill her. Instantly, a wave of guilt rushes over me. I try to see where she goes, but then our car hits a solid structure in the street.

My brain finds this a good time to point out the unstoppable-force paradox: *What happens when an unstoppable force meets an immovable object?*

I immediately see the error in my thinking since our cab turns out to be entirely stoppable. The crash is forceful and propels the taxi driver straight through the car's windshield, out of sight. His right shoe is left sitting on top of the dashboard, as the last reminder that this was indeed his taxi.

And his life.

I am in the rear wearing my seat belt, and, although it saves my life, it breaks several of my ribs on impact. My face smashes against the back of the front seat, and I taste warm leather, something I will remember the rest of my life. I try to see outside, but blood is running in my eyes, which is scaring the shit out of me. Everything becomes a red blur. A nasty thought pierces through the fog: *This is one obstacle you did not find your way around, did you?*

The car has wrapped itself around what turns out to be a Buddhist shrine, one of many in the streets of Bangkok. This simple fact does not help matters at all. The Thai are hyper-sensitive when it comes to their places of worship. Sacred ground and all that.

I try to open the car door, but it will not budge. I smell gasoline fumes and immediately agonize whether I will burn alive in this car wreck in a city far from home. I feel extremely nauseous and rest my head for just a moment against the front seat to find my bearings. I feel like I might throw up. But before I can do so, I feel hands pulling at my arms and legs. *People are trying to save me*, is the hopeful but rather naïve thought that pops into my mind.

Next thing I know, a clenched fist hits my jaw. The surprise of this event has more punch than the actual pain it causes.

This does not make sense. No sense at all. I am a victim.

Before I can ascertain who has hit me and why, I feel a sharp object stabbing me twice in the left thigh. Two deep thrusts in exactly the same spot. It occurs to me that I've never felt a knife cut into my flesh except for the harmless nick in a finger while cooking. I can now confirm that the pain is excruciating. It feels like nothing for a second until the red hot pain sears through the wound.

I cry out in torment and anger.

I hear police sirens very close by, and the angry crowd surrounding the car seems to hesitate for a moment. But then it moves closer again, pulsating in and out of my view. People are shouting a word I do not understand. The police will later tell me it means *child killer.*

My hand instinctively tries to stop the bleeding of my leg. I can feel blood gushing out of the laceration. I black out for a second or so. When I open my eyes again, I see a single Thai police officer standing at a distance of less than a meter from my face but with his back to me. I move my head slightly in an attempt to get a better view, but this sends a bolt of pain all the way down my spine.

This opens a new avenue of agonizing worry. I wonder whether I'm paralyzed from the neck down. I'm trying to feel my toes, but my brain cannot seem to send them the right command.

I notice now that the cop is holding a handgun and is pointing it straight at the mob of people surrounding the crash site. He's shouting quick words in Thai. I can sense from his tone that he is way out of his depth here. He does not sound confident at all that he can keep the crowd from tearing me apart.

Not confident at all.

His short warnings are met by the most guttural outbursts of anger I've ever heard in my life. It's clear that this crowd wants me dead. A memory of reading about lynch mobs at crash incidents in Thailand flashes through my brain. Very helpful.

I hear a gun blast very close to my left ear when the officer fires a warning shot. My ear is ringing, and my head hurts like hell. I am convinced now that the leaking gasoline will catch fire or the angry posse will finally push through. Whatever gets to me first.

A strange thought occurs to me. *I swear I will stop drinking and better myself if I make it out of here alive.* This is when my consciousness says, *Enough, already,* and I pass out.

I have no idea how long I'm gone or what happens to me. I drift in and out of an uneasy sleep. The moments I am awake, I think I am in a hospital, but I cannot be sure. I get a glimpse of light-green painting on the walls and a lot of white neon lights above me.

And I dream.

It is difficult to describe the deeply feverish nature of the dreams. I am unhinged. It feels as if continental drift below the surface of my consciousness causes my tectonic plates to collide. A tidal wave of unsettling images is flooding the seaboards of my sanity. This is one fragment of a dream I will remember till the day I die.

A massive battleship fueled by a colossal reactor engine cuts through the ocean. Somehow, I just know that it's the world's largest destroyer and it is tried-and-true invincible.

Then, out of nowhere, the war cruiser is hit amidships by a ridiculously small torpedo, the size of a Cuban cigar.

The ship is so large that at first, the hit goes unnoticed, with just a light tremble rippling up and down the five gargantuan decks of the superstructure.

Eventually, a sailor notices a small hull breach, but he hesitates for a moment before reporting it, as he does not wish to be ridiculed.

Normal operations are barely disturbed as the crew executes the emergency procedure for this type of minor incident. The ship itself seems to mock this poor attempt at a threat and only reluctantly can be made to slow down, as if it has a mind of its own.

After swift repairs, the captain confidently gives the command from the bridge to resume cruising speed, and the warship accelerates until it again cuts through the waves at an amazing one hundred knots.

Nothing happens for hours.

But then, the pipes with engine-cooling water unexpectedly show leakage and have to be shut down. As a consequence, the core of the reactor heats up until it is flaming red hot.

Without cooling, the reactor eventually melts down, and deadly radiation spreads out from the belly of the ship.

Everybody on board is exposed.

Other vessels are hours away, and, instead of a green Exit sign, the word "Hubris" is displayed in red neon above the only emergency gate. There is no escape.

Thousands of souls are lost at sea.

I wake up in a sweat with a deep-rooted feeling of trepidation. My leg hurts like hell, my nose feels broken, and I have a hard time breathing. I still taste the warm leather of the cab seat in my mouth. I hear noises surrounding my bed, and I open my eyes.

The first thing I see is the little girl. This time she's wearing a bright green dress. She is standing at the left side of my bed, and she's holding a small bouquet of wildflowers. Her face is serious, but she does not look angry. I blink to make sure I am fully conscious. The girl is holding the hand of her mother, who's smiling down at me in a sweet, forgiving way.

I frantically look up and down at the girl, and I see that she has a bandage on her right knee.

Never before in my life have I felt such relief. It turns out that Boonsri—that's the girl's name—was indeed catapulted from her bike but then landed just meters further in a makeshift clothing stall in the street. The racks full of colorful textiles broke her fall, and she was unharmed, apart from a nasty cut on her right knee.

While I was unconscious, more police had come to cordon off the car wreck. Within that sealed perimeter, they managed to free me from the demolished cab. An ambulance then swiftly evacuated me to Bangkok's Bumrungrad International Hospital, at the far end of Sukhumvit Street.

The taxi driver died instantly upon hitting the shrine head first. The autopsy performed yesterday revealed he had opiates in his bloodstream and was found guilty—posthumously—of reckless driving under the influence of illegal substances. If he had made it out alive, he would have gotten the death penalty under Thai drug laws.

The perpetrator who had knifed me twice had not been captured; he ran off into the crowded streets. Same with the guy who broke my nose.

Four days later, I find myself aboard a Lear Jet 55 in a medical air ambulance, leased by the insurance firm, to repatriate me back to Switzerland for treatment of the sustained leg injury and my severe concussion. On this hospital bed at thirty thousand feet up in the air, it feels like I have a new lease on life.

I am humbled by what has happened, and I'm trying to deal with the guilt over the taxi driver's death. Yes, he'd been on drugs, but if I had not pushed him over the edge, all of this could have been avoided, and he would be showing his great city to a tourist right now. I will have to live with that. Even deeper guilt is there for all the time wasted. I have been on the wrong track for a very long time, and this car crash was my come-to-Jesus moment.

I have a new appreciation for life now. It is amazing that something that nearly killed me can instill such a powerful sense that a richer existence might now be in reach. I don't need to be the overbearing, opinionated alpha male any longer. Enough already with this ego-driven narcissistic bullshit. I don't need to be paid a lot of money for being an arrogant, high-handed asshole. I don't need to fly business class and have my vulnerable ego stroked with a Platinum Frequent Flyer card and pretty flight attendants bringing me drink after drink. I do not have to treat people like shit to demonstrate my own importance.

All this time, I've been terrified of facing myself. I escaped in frantic diversions like traveling and working. And drinking, of course—let's not forget the drinking. Booze has been my instrument of choice for self-sabotage for so many years. This guilt for time wasted can now act as a call from within, a guide to a better me.

Cruising at forty thousand feet, I cannot help but smile while flipping through Bangkok's only English newspaper, *The Nation*. I instantly recognize the pictures of Katya and Vlad, the Russian lovers apparently taken into custody yesterday at the Bangkok Marriott and brought before the city's 2nd District Court on charges of sex in a public place and indecent exposure. A German woman who found herself trapped in the elevator with the promiscuous couple filed a formal complaint, and the rest is history.

CHAPTER 19

LIFE'S PARADOX

BY CATHERINE LAVORTER

The three of us sat on the wrought-iron chairs on the terrace outside my office, overlooking the water. Peter sipped iced tea we had poured him from a cooled carafe. For a while, we just enjoyed the evening silence and the tranquil view of two white swans floating by.

Dusk was settling over the mountains, until we no longer could make out the quayside on the other side of the lake where Sisi—short for Empress Elisabeth of Austria—was stabbed to death in the fall of 1898. Peter broke the silence by suggesting we should maybe discuss his Bangkok story.

Adaline for one, remained quiet, no doubt cautious after her frustrating attempt in the last session to engage with him on his earlier Singapore piece. So

I took the cue and said, "Peter, I was shocked to learn about the accident and the little girl. Did all of this happen for real?"

"Yes, the facts occurred just as I described them, back when I was still drinking. But I was living in a daze, at the time. I was completely out of touch with myself."

"Yet with this story, you've found the courage, long after the facts, to breathe meaning into that whole incident by facing the pain again and writing it up like a confession. No mean feat, Peter."

"Well, I guess it finally led to some form of redemption that was long overdue," he responded. "Just the fact of replaying the frantic scenes in Bangkok from an alternate vantage point felt like a purge."

"Alternate in what sense?"

"Well, by putting the events in the context of not living up to my true potential. In our last session, we agreed that what I had felt all this time was guilt for not being the person I could have been. It felt good to confess to that and to get it off my chest."

I understood that he used his stories to integrate whatever "Aha!" moments we had in our therapy sessions, but, still, it triggered a question in me about how he used his base instincts. "The way that the story unfolds and builds up to its conclusions fascinates me. The dream sequences, the multi-layering and the double entendre in your stories makes me think that you come to insights and conclusions based upon hunches and gut feelings, rather than just clear thinking. Is that correct?"

"Funny you should mention this, Catherine. Yes, it is obvious that my inspiration comes from somewhere else than just my thinking mind."

I was acutely aware of the fact that he had called me by my given name, "Catherine," for the first time ever. I wondered what to make of that. Much to my embarrassment, I could feel myself starting to blush. I hoped he and Adaline would not notice. Best to focus and continue.

"That confirms exactly what I thought. You pour your very soul into these stories. They have this Kafkaesque quality, which reflects your inner turmoil. But their authenticity for sure mirrors who you really are, and so you should trust your conclusions and act upon them."

He nodded and looked out over the water for a long, pensive moment before returning his attention back to me. He did not speak.

I continued. "In our very first session, you wanted me to cure you from your incessant thinking, right? You pleaded for me to help you find a safe place within yourself where you could be free from your own mind."

"Sure did, Doc."

We were back to *Doc*. Somehow this felt like a mild bee sting. Him calling me "Catherine" must have been a lapse. But at some level, I'd liked it, and now it made me wonder why he'd stopped.

I quickly brushed away these ridiculous thoughts. Transference was at play here, clearly. I tried to regain my professional composure, more than a bit annoyed with myself.

"Well, Peter, on the one hand, you overthink matters, but, on the other hand, you have a remarkable sixth sense. What you need is to learn to leverage both."

"Sixth sense?"

"Yes. When faced with decisions in any complex situation, try first to form a working hypothesis with that intuition and then to use your natural-born reason to do a reality check."

"Let me guess: My writing is a fast route to that intuition, right?"

"I would even say that it is the only way for you to bypass your mind and your five senses and perceive a deeper reality. Like I said, it is literally a sixth sense."

"You're telling me that I have this power that I do not know about?'

"To quote Canadian writer Malcolm Gladwell: 'There can be as much value in the blink of an eye as in months of rational analysis.' I think, Peter, that you are very apt at reading signs and tapping into your inner wisdom in unorthodox ways."

Peter seemed fascinated with that premise, so I continued.

"Intuition, as you seem to command it, is a powerful bridge between emotion and thought. It's so subtle that you don't even realize it is working for you. Indeed, you seem to be unaware of this hidden talent."

It had gotten completely dark now, with the top of Mont Blanc bathing in the soft glow of the crescent moon. As it was getting chilly, I was about to suggest we move inside. But then Peter said, "There were two different versions of me in the Bangkok story, right? Before the accident, my ego controlled me completely, but then, after the crash, a more genuine side of me emerged. At least in the story, that is."

"What do you mean with 'at least in the story'?" I asked.

"Well, what happened in reality is that the humble version of me did not really show up after the crash. Back then, I did not come to the same insights as I did now. Back when all of it happened, I remained very much the smug, self-important business type, and I remember going back to drinking as fast as I could, right after I got back home."

Once again, he had thrown me off balance. I could have sworn that the contrition he wrote about so convincingly in the Bangkok story had been a genuine feeling he'd experienced at the time of the accident. Now it turned out that, while the event itself was real, the ensuing emotions emerged only now, four years later, when he unlocked them in his narrative.

Adaline stood up to get us some blankets that I store in my office. I did not want to stop his train of thought, and so I urged him to go on.

"I almost died in that cab, and yet, as frightening as the whole incident was, it did not open my eyes back then. How can it be that only now, being sober and reliving it four years later, I am able to see how that crash really affected me and how I was responsible for it, really?" He paused for a moment, and then added, "It is amazing how time works, isn't it? It seems the past is not entirely done with until you look at it with your full consciousness."

I decided not to let him in on my surprise about the time lapse between the event on the one hand and his real sentiments on the other. Instead I said "Sobriety is a gift that keeps on giving."

He looked at me questioningly.

"By banning alcohol from your life, your attitude shifted from hubris and overall superiority, all the way down to humility and a complete absence of hypocrisy. And indeed, a new alertness came over you. You've come to see things clearly, even things that are far in the past. Sometimes, it seems that reality does not exist until you're looking at it with your full attention."

He was glowing upon hearing this. He wanted so much to believe that he had changed for the better, that he was becoming a new person.

"I think you now want to feel fully accountable," I said. "Because you know that, in the end, only rigorous honesty can make you whole again. Addiction, after all, is nothing if not an attempt to live life outside of accountability."

"Well, it sure is an eye opener how my not drinking can bring truth to the surface. I'm finally able to distill a drop of meaning from an otherwise lifeless episode." He looked at me intensely. "What I mean is that I'd never have thought that anything good could come from that absolute low point in my life. Trying to make sense of it felt like extracting water from a rock. And yet now I feel a sense of satisfaction that I made it through that horrible period of uncontrollable drinking. I've come out a different man."

"You call your drinking years 'a lifeless time.' 'Lifeless' is indeed a good word to describe the deadening quality of the addictive experience." It was important that he did not step into the trap of romanticizing the whole drinking episode but rather saw it for what it really was. "You were on a truly hopeless carousel ride, but you got yourself off just in time."

"Yes I did, Doc."

"Your storytelling about the events leading up to the taxi accident captured the absolute insanity of the ego state that drove you to be a high-functioning alcoholic with a crazy compulsion to excel in business and stand out from the crowd. Just so you could stay in denial of your fear of dying and of your guilt for wasting the best years of your life."

"You use the word 'compulsion,'" he said. "That makes it sound like I was a helpless victim. Let's be honest here: It would have been fair only if I had died in that cab, instead of that poor taxi driver."

"No point in going down that route. In fact, you've allowed that series of unfortunate events to transform you; that, in the end, is what counts."

He looked at me quizzically. It was clear I had to spell it out using logic, the language he understood best. "Three things happened there in Bangkok. First, the crash itself made you realize that you'd been astray, thinking only about yourself and that what happened was exactly what you deserved, as you put it. Then the dream you had in the hospital about the unsinkable ship that in the end proved to be vulnerable after all, that was a significant turning point because it put a big fat hole in your denial mechanism. It made you realize that you were not invincible. That you weren't special or immortal. And finally, the fact that the little girl turned out to be unharmed against all odds, had enormous symbolic value. A second chance like that, you only get once in life."

I paused for a moment. "Do not disrespect a gift like that by concluding that it should have been you dying. That would mean you missed the point completely."

"Yeah, alright. I see what you mean. I need to take this opportunity with both hands and make something of the rest of my life. I am just not clear what that is, exactly."

"Throughout our therapy sessions, you've been integrating all these discoveries into a new and improved version of yourself. Do not underestimate what's been happening here. Remember the concept of alchemy, turning base metals into gold? You've been turning your misery into priceless insights."

He quietly acknowledged my words as he looked out to the darkness of the lake. In turn, I also took in the surreal view before us, with the snow-covered mountain-tops mirrored by the moonlight into the blackness of Lake Geneva. Glancing at Adaline, I noticed that she was wearing a lovely dress with a subtle polka dot background that was exactly right for this moment. She listened while smiling demurely, and I could not help but wonder how there was a lot more to her than meets the eye.

I had grown very fond of Adaline Vikander, on both a professional and a personal level, and I was seriously considering hiring her on a permanent basis, once her internship was completed. She was a diamond in the rough as far as I was concerned.

A couple of minutes passed by without any of us speaking. Then Peter said, "Ladies, do you recall the story about my swimming further and further away from shore in the Caribbean, wondering what the point was of it all?"

"Sure, it was one of the first vignettes you wrote, right after we started therapy," I said. "I remember

189

also that your conclusion was to aim high, aim for the meaning of your life. Am I right?"

"Well yes, but even now, I am still looking for that same sense of purpose. I have come to learn a great deal about myself since then, yet I still feel that I'm constantly circling back to that same question: Why?"

"Peter, this might indeed feel like déjà vu, but I want to point out that there is a difference now compared to back then."

"What's that, then?" he asked.

"This time around, you're taking yourself much less seriously. There is less drama, less self-pity."

"I guess it's true that I have come to see that my circumstances are not as unique as I thought initially. We're all in this boat together. I am just a man, like any other."

"Yes, and you have started using irony as a weapon against the absurdity. The way you talk and write clearly reflects that you take yourself with a large pinch of salt now."

"If with 'irony,' you mean the realization that we are all creating our own truth of what life is all about, than I agree. It's clearly up to us to make it count, because for sure, the universe will not do it for us. We have no choice but to make the best of it."

"Yes, and in your stories, you detach yourself from your own importance and observe what happens with a sense of humor."

"Humor? I use humor?" His reaction in itself was very funny, and I couldn't help but smile. Peter was and would always be the archetypal intellectual.

"You have learned to master irony in the sense that you have come to see your own predicament as amusing rather than terrifying. You now understand that your disconcertedness with existence cannot be cured, and yet it is not insanity. It is what we shrinks call 'normal neurotic existence'. For us humans, it is simply impossible not to be in despair, but the key is to be aware of it and use it to enrich our lives. The fact that life is transient makes it so much more precious."

"Is that not turning things upside down? Life is better because it is ending?"

"To quote Kierkegaard: 'Whoever has learned to be anxious in the right way has learned the ultimate.'"

"If that's the case, why is it that I am still so preoccupied with death?"

"Sure, you still talk about your fear of death, but you've started to see that this is, in fact, the very backbone of a well-lived life. Anxiety has stirred up your spiritual life because you have started to take your struggle with the human condition seriously, rather than drinking it away like you used to do."

Intrigued, he urged me to go on. "Without that anxiety, you would not have regained your sensitivity to life. Your profound sense of unease keeps you on your toes and makes you work up the courage every single day to reach a more positive state of mind. We discussed courage in our last session. Anxiety is the basic experience of the paradox of life."

"Paradox?"

"How to purposefully deal with our sense of disorientation in a universe believed to be absurd. In other words, how to approach life in an optimistic way and enjoy it despite our obvious vulnerability and uncertainty."

"But I'm stuck at that very point. How can I neglect for one minute that my very existence is built on a swamp? Should I fool myself into believing everything is okay?"

Before I had a chance to speak, Adaline said, "Peter, in your Curacao story, you pictured yourself as a small red dot in a vast blue body of water, just like Google Maps visualizes earth from outer space, right?"

Peter was somewhat taken aback by her unexpected intervention. "Yes?"

"That is what is known as the galactic perspective," she said. "Looking down at ourselves from that height, it makes us feel like we are but microscopic specs in the vast expanse of the cosmos." She continued with confidence. "That's when the absurdity paradox is at its extreme. From a cosmic perspective, it's very hard to fathom that we as mortal human beings amongst countless other life forms can amount to anything in the greater scheme of things. All our efforts seem foolish and trivial, and whether we exist or not doesn't seem to make a great difference."

"Galactic. I see." Peter said this in a slightly mocking tone. Adaline did not seem to notice the sneer, or she excelled at ignoring it.

"I would advise that you distance yourself from that universal perspective," she said, "because it only drains vitality from real life through endless abstraction. In the end, it would appear that nothing matters and all good things are just vanities in the bigger picture. In short, life is a bitch and then you die."

She was speaking with authority and not holding back one bit. I wondered where this was coming from. After all, she was all of twenty-nine years of age. But it was exactly her young perspective that made her examples and analogies so refreshing. I was trying to decide for myself whether her words sounded more captivating because of, or despite, her ravishing looks. Peter surely looked completely mesmerized with her, and yet I wondered whether he really took her seriously.

Adaline plowed ahead. "You are a businessman so you must do a lot of work on your laptop, right?"

Peter could only nod.

"Well, then you're familiar with both Word and PDF file formats, right?" It was clear from his expression that Peter did not know where this was going, and I was wondering about that myself. "Well to me, real life is like Word. You can see the spelling errors and wrong paragraph indenting, but that's okay because you know you can still change things. Text in a Word format can still be processed, while a PDF freezes all imperfections for eternity. What the galactic perspective does is to wrap up all the nitty gritty details that make life real in some glossy and detached format that can no longer be adapted to changing realities."

Brilliant. She was unstoppable.

"Come back down to earth now, and zoom in on the present moment. You are with us here on this lovely evening. Breathe in the fresh alpine air, look at the majestic Mont Blanc and the icy glacier water of Lake Geneva." She paused and then concluded. "Just be here!"

I could see that Peter fully understood what she was saying but rather than acknowledging her, he said with a half-smile, "You mean I'm not here, then?"

I made a mental note to investigate what it was that made Peter time and again want to frustrate Adaline in her attempts to help him. Adaline, however, was unfazed.

"I am just trying to get my point across, Peter," she said. "You are physically here, but mostly, you are stuck in your head." She clearly was not intimidated by him.

At all. "There is something very noxious in stepping too far back from life and only contemplating its meaning all the time. What you need to do now is to de-reflect; you have done enough thinking for one lifetime. You should grab life with both hands and re-engage with it."

It seemed Adaline had saved up all her thoughts just for today. She had lit up the night air with a fireworks of relevance. Funnily enough, Peter suddenly seemed to come to the urgent realization he needed to be more accommodating toward her.

"You have made some very fine points here, Adaline, and I want to thank you for that," he said, trying hard to find the right words. "I think what you are saying is that even if things do not nicely hang together into some unified grand scheme, that's okay, as long as they matter to me. Like my music and my books, or the fact that I love a good philosophical discussion. Those things matter to me, even if by themselves they cannot explicitly give me the meaning of life."

Adaline nodded and smiled a beautiful smile. She looked up at the clock and said, "According to the Buddha, one must immerse oneself in the river of life and let all questions drift away. I happen to agree. I think life just happens to be and requires no reason."

She had managed this very competently. The hour was up.

CHAPTER 20

THOUSAND WEDDINGS

BY PETER BAER

Although it's Saturday, I wake up at six AM from an uneasy sleep and look at my mobile phone. I see that I have five missed calls and one voicemail. The country code of the incessant night caller is +91, which is India. I'm wondering what this might be about as I dial my voicemail.

I listen to the elaborate message, which is delivered in Indian English with heavily trilled Rs. When the content of the voice message hits home, my mind races back to my last trip to India, now six months ago. The memory is so vivid that it seems I am instantly back over there.

Early May is a great time to come to Bangalore. A balmy breeze welcomes me as I close my eyes and take a deep breath outside of Karnataka International Airport. The glorious fragrance of black cardamom and holy basil in the warm and humid Indian air is as unique as it gets. Just like a master sommelier can tell his Grand Crus wines in a blind tasting, a traveling man like me knows his cities just by breathing in the air. Moscow is gasoline, Beijing is smog, but Bangalore is heaven.

I am dead tired. After an eleven-hour flight from Europe, our Airbus-320 was kept from docking at the airport terminal because a stray dog was moving freely about on the tarmac. It took two hours before the control tower finally gave us permission to taxi to the gate.

The *Hindustan Times* of tomorrow will cover the delay, stating matter-of-factly that the airport's GHOST Team—as in Ground Handling Operations Safety—had been unable to locate the proper procedure in their operations manual on how to capture the frightened animal.

It's become exceedingly clear to me from curious incidents like the one with the stray dog that India is destined for spiritual rather than practical greatness. Fast and efficient seems to go against the grain in this country. Struggling along is the natural flow of things.

Indian locals are known to happily meander and stray off course in their very own dimension of time. To the world, IST means Indian Standard Time, but when you get to see the way things are done here on the ground, you'll see that it is actually India Stretched Time. The attitude here toward time is fluid and relaxed, to say the least, because of their cyclical view. When you expect to live multiple times through reincarnation, there is no real need to stick to the clock. If things do not work out this time around, you can always try again in a next life. Time does not hold the importance it does in the West, because, here in India, there will always be a fresh start.

As a foreigner, it takes some getting used to the fact that deadlines here are not absolute. But I love this country because its circumstances simply force you to take a philosophical stance in life. Although we tend to look down upon their funny, half-baked approach to things, Indians seem to capture the essence of human existence better than we do.

The Buddha taught that all things and beings are impermanent, and, therefore, any attachment to them is a source of unhappiness. Indians eat and breathe this "life is life" attitude and attach less importance to the illusion of control than we do, taking joy in letting things unfold.

Thinking about this, I'm reminded of Fiona Apple's song "Container," in which she captures the crux of life's contingent nature: "I have only one thing to do and that's to be the wave that I am and then sink back into the ocean."

I step into a taxi and smile when I see a huge billboard that says "Incredible India," the aptly chosen tagline of the Ministry of Tourism's advertising campaign, designed to welcome the inbound traveler.

Incredible, indeed.

This time around, I am in Bangalore to hire a new India country manager. The previous one was detained a week ago by the Fraud Investigation Office on charges of collusion with local officials. Turns out he paid "speed money" to get faster clearance through Indian bureaucracy. A rather unfortunate misinterpretation of the sense of urgency I had imposed upon him.

My company operates a zero-tolerance policy when it comes to corruption, so I had no choice but to take a firm stance. This type of firing is not uncommon among multinationals in India, but it's a first for me. Anyway, I want to move on and reboot the entire organization. I have my work cut out for me these coming days. But this trip is special also for a more pleasant reason.

I have been kindly invited to attend the marriage of Anika, the sophisticated and elegant young woman who is my local operations manager here. Her name means "grace," and she has a regal air about her, with her long black hair always done up and her dark-brown, almond-shaped eyes. Her soft voice demands respect while her coy smile makes me forget sometimes that we're in a place of business.

She's been the first in her family to earn a Ph.D. at the Indian Institute of Science, an absolute top university, and she's proven herself to be invaluable to the team in the two years she's been with us. She's an ambitious and proud young woman, which makes her choice of a husband all the more intriguing.

The marriage, an inter-caste affair, is somewhat of a controversy. Anika originates from Brahmin lineage, the upper-crust social class in India. For some time now, she's had her mind set on marrying Anirudha, a young man from the backward Dalit caste. Dalit, meaning oppressed, is the caste of Untouchables, the fifth group beyond the four-fold classification of the Indian population.

Anirudha is an equally striking young man who goes through life undaunted by his low-born heritage. He's strong willed, and Anika is what he wants.

They met a little over a year ago when she visited the hospital where he works as a security guard. Struck by love, Anirudha did not hesitate one minute to ask Anika out on a date. His sheer determination won her over, and they fell in love. Variations of this Bollywood-type story have circulated in the office ever since, and everyone was delighted when they decided to tie the knot.

I have seen the couple together a couple of times at company functions, and, to me, they seem a match made in heaven. They have eyes only for each other and do not care what social-compatibility code they are supposed to adhere to. I am happy for them, and my gut says, "Go for it!"

But things are all but straightforward here. Caste fanatics raise hell whenever an upper-caste woman marries a Dalit man because she will bear—unavoidably—a lower-caste heir, thereby contaminating her social class. This sort of mismatch often leads to violence. That's why many marriages are still pre-arranged by the parents based on caste and often even horoscope sign, exactly to avoid this kind of unfortunate outcome of real love. The cynic in me understands, but the romantic says, "Screw it."

It all seems hypocritical. Caste politics here at play are about masculine ego more than anything else. If a man of a higher station marries a Dalit woman, he is praised for his benevolence; he is said to have uplifted her. If an upper-caste woman marries a Dalit man, all hell breaks loose.

So, I'm still ambivalent toward this. The last thing I need is for this quagmire to seep through into the office space and pollute the already-delicate working environment. My attending the wedding means taking a clear position, and I need to be absolutely sure this will not open a can of worms.

But when I arrive at the office, Anika is all smiles, and she goes to great lengths to assure me I should not worry. Their two families have had intense discussions and have agreed, in the end, to dismiss all outside criticism and fully support the union in the name of true love. And to be fully validated under India's Special Marriage Act, the couple has put up a Notice of Intent at the Registrar's Office to publicly declare their engagement to be married as an inter-caste couple. Much like we in Europe would put up a sign on a piece of land declaring our intention to build a house.

Love overcomes all obstacles, it seems, with a little help from the government in this particular case. I decide for myself I am fine with this state of affairs. I feel relieved and even buoyed.

Anika and Anirudha will not be the only couple in Bangalore to be joined in matrimony this week. This coming Friday, the city has one thousand weddings scheduled on the occasion of Akshaya Tritiya, a most auspicious day in the Hindu lunar calendar. According to mythology, the sacred river Ganges descended to the earth from heaven on this holy day.

All of Bangalore's wedding halls, all of its ceremonial music bands, and all of its priests have been booked a year in advance for this glorious occasion. A thousand proud fathers are looking forward to giving their daughters away in marriage on this enchanted day because that is believed to bring great prosperity not only to the couples but also to the entire families.

The city vibrates with the preparations of a thousand nuptials. It is hard to imagine ten weddings or a hundred. But a thousand couples getting married on the same day is beyond comprehension. The anticipation is palpable in the streets and in the parks of the city. Rich and poor are getting ready to celebrate the good fortune of their sons and daughters on this saintly date, assured of divine protection by a multitude of Hindu deities.

Usually, I am all business, but this gets to me. I am absolutely thrilled to be part of this because it feels like an antidote to the cynicism that is so pervasive in Western society today. People here are getting ready to celebrate life without reservations and are prepared to go all in, like there's no tomorrow.

The big day presents itself under a scorching sun, set high in an ultramarine sky. As I'm driven in a taxi to the wedding venue, I see a city full of exuberance. Music and flowers are everywhere, and literally everyone is dressed for the occasion. Even the beggars seem to own an Auspicious Day suit for a rare lunar juncture like this. Just for one day, everyone manages to forget the harsh realities of life in Bengaluru. There are higher things at stake now.

I feel on top of the world when I arrive at Anika's posh wedding venue, the Leela Palace Kempinski, which is by far the grandest hotel in the whole of Karnataka state. To make guests feel welcome, at the entrance, young girls are scattering flower petals, and boys are carrying metal torches emanating clouds of incense.

Two colossal elephant-shaped flower sculptures, made from thousands of white jasmine flowers, guard the hotel entrance. Jasmine is claimed to be the favorite flower of Lord Vishnu, and its sweet smell is believed to calm the nerves of the bride.

Before entering, I look in wonder at the Leela's staggering architecture, which is inspired by the Royal Palace of Mysore, the official residence of the Maharajas who used to rule this princely state. I am in awe of its grandeur while I cross the lobby and follow a signpost which has "Anika & Anirudha" written in golden letters on purple cloth.

The ceremonial area itself is composed of a beautifully elevated terrace with an opulent pool full of daffodils, sitting on nine acres of lush tropical gardens within the hotel walls. It's clear that all the guests have been made aware of my coming, and I feel thoroughly stared at. The family of the bride considers it a big deal that I, Anika's hierarchical superior at her place of work, would celebrate this life milestone in their midst.

I am invited to walk through an impressive arcaded gallery and to step onto the grand terrace amidst the clangs of ceremonial cymbals. My name is proclaimed in a deep voice by a towering, bearded man in a black ceremonial dress wearing a richly bejeweled turban. I feel very self-conscious but decide to play along with the role of distinguished guest, although I would have preferred to be observing from the gallery.

The bride looks absolutely gorgeous in a traditional red wedding sari, red being considered the most propitious color for a holy occasion like this one. Her hair is done in an elegant waterfall braid, which makes her look both sexy and chaste.

Throughout the ceremony, the handsome groom cannot stop looking at his bride. He's clearly over his head in love, and that simple fact puts a smile on everybody's face. It's strange to think there was ever any doubt about these two getting married. Fate clearly has put its foot down here.

The couple exchanges marigold garlands of flowers and thread, symbolizing happiness. Just as the thread never leaves the flowers, even when they lose their luster with time, the married couple swears to never leave each other, through all the ups and downs of life.

I'm actually enjoying the Indian wedding decorum more than I thought I would. Especially the climax, the equivalent to our "I do," is a pleasure to watch. It is called *Saptapadi* or Seven Vows, which bride and groom recite to each other while taking seven steps due South.

Everybody cheers after the vows have been taken, while the families of both bride and groom stand united, with absolutely no visible distinction between them. Without a doubt, Anika's parents are footing the bill for this extravaganza, which I think is a great gesture of open-mindedness and a tribute to modern-day India.

Finally, all the guests get seated along heavy wooden tables in the long shadows cast by two rows of silver poplar trees. Giant crystal candelabras with long white candles sit upon the stretched tables. The newlyweds take their places at the head of the main table in two statuesque antique chairs, decorated with colorful ethnic cushions and drapes.

I relax and take a deep breath as I look around me, holding a bohemia crystal glass of tangerine juice and smelling the abundant lavender. This place seems unreal. We could very well be a millennium back in the past, I'd bet the place would look exactly like this. I feel like I have been transported back to a more profound era when things were more authentic somehow.

All the men, including me, are dressed in ethnic *Dhoti Sherwani*, a long coat-like garment which makes me feel part of an ancient protocol, reserved for the privileged Indian aristocracy of days long gone. As an after-ceremony, *mehndi* or henna patterns are applied by the sisters of Anika to her hands and feet, which give this whole scene a primeval touch. Tradition has it that the bride should not work in her marital home until her Mehndi fades.

Anika has been aware that I have an interest in philosophy and spiritualism and has seated me next to her great-grandfather, Mr. Lakshmi Kaur, who is known throughout Karnataka as the "Healer of the Soul."

The old man is a living legend, renowned for his deep expertise in Vipassanā, an age-old meditation technique to see things as they really are through self-observation, resulting in a balanced mind full of peace and compassion.

Honoring me with a place at the main table, next to the wise old man in this most wonderful of settings has been Anika's very personal gift to me and a thank-you for my moral support through the difficult time leading up to this special day. This feels truly reciprocal, and I accept her gift with gratitude and enthusiasm.

During and after a splendid *chaat* table, with an incredible array of deliciously spiced South-Indian dishes, I have a mind-baffling conversation with Mr. Kaur.

"It's a pleasure meeting you today at this glorious occasion of your great-granddaughter's wedding, sir. May I ask how old you are?"

"I could be ninety-four. No way to be certain," he responded.

"That would make you exactly twice my age."

"Age and time are an illusion. Now is all there ever is. "

"Sir, with all due respect, my whole life revolves around my calendar," I said. "Without time, I'd be lost."

"Past and future exist only as thoughts in the present. There never was, nor will there ever be any other experience than present experience."

"But I always feel like the clock is ticking and I should hurry because time is running out on me."

"The clock is not ticking because there is no clock. Time is a construct of the mind, not an entity that exists in nature," he said.

"It is true that I have trouble living in the present; I carry my past with me, and I worry about the future."

"Do not resist this moment. Accept it as if it is exactly as you have chosen it."

"But there is so much I would like to fix about my life."

"You want to change your life situation, not your life. Your life is your essence, which is already perfect. Stop doing and focus on being. Let the present just unfold."

"I'm sorry, but I'm afraid I do not get it. Why is the now so important?"

"You are walking along a path at night, surrounded by a thick fog. But you have a powerful searchlight that cuts through the fog and that creates a narrow, clear space in front of you. The fog is your life situation, which includes past and future. The searchlight is your alertness, your conscious presence. The clear space is the now."

"A powerful image, that is. So you are saying that a focus on the now brings clarity. It's true that my mind is always straying. It is absolutely restless—that is just who I am."

"You are not your mind," he said. "Do not identify with your thoughts—observe them, and let them go. Do not follow them."

"I am sorry, but what am I then, if not my mind?" I asked.

"Picture a lake high up in the mountains. You are the deep and permanent stillness at the bottom of the lake. Your thoughts and emotions are the wrinkles and waves on the surface of the water."

We stop talking, and we just sit in absolute silence for at least twenty minutes. Mr. Kaur signals me to stay quiet every time he sees I am about to ask another question. To him, quietness is a natural state. I realize he does this to give me the time needed to let it all sink in. He masters silence just as he masters words.

I feel there is great value in what he said, but at the same time, I feel frustrated because it feels evanescent. It seems impossible to capture its essence within my predefined European frame of mind.

Dusk is setting in, and the sky turns amethyst. Eventually, I feel I have to say something. "Well, at your age, you must have attended many weddings, I guess?"

"This is the wedding."

I smile at this perfect ending to a perfect day, realizing that I have a long way to go before I can begin to understand what the old man is trying to convey to me. My mind actually stops thinking while night falls over the Leela Palace Gardens. I'm watching how

Anirudha invites Anika for the closing dance, and it feels like I am experiencing this in a trance.

Incredible India.

I find myself returning to the present day, still sitting up straight in bed, holding my mobile phone to my ear. Just like a photo is the capturing of past light which we can see in the present, a memory is the impression of a past experience on our present self. That trip to Bangalore has made a deep impact on me, and I've only just now come to realize how deep, so many months later.

What triggered this vivid flashback is, of course, the voicemail from Mr. Pannerselvam, Commissioner of Police of Bengaluru, telling me that his troopers found my name and number as an emergency contact on the phone of Mrs. Anika Garbinder-Pillai. As it turns out, Anika came home from work yesterday evening, and she found a group of male university graduates from her own upper-level Brahim caste protesting in front of her house. They were in the process of distributing pamphlets of their "Campaign Against Inter-Caste Marriage," claiming that boys from downtrodden communities who deliberately targeted wealthy girls should be stoned to death.

God knows why they had to come to her house today, so many months after the controversial marriage. When Anika saw their provocative signboards, she angrily told them to go away. For a moment there, it looked like her assertiveness would actually drive them off. But then one of the agitators noticed Anika's belly, clearly showing her five-month pregnancy.

Anirudha was at work, just starting his night shift at the hospital. He was happy and completely unaware while Anika was beaten with pipe wrenches and wrecking bars by the cultured class activists until she and her unborn child died from what the forensic pathologist would later call a blunt force trauma.

CHAPTER 21

BACK INTO THE FLOW OF THINGS

BY CATHERINE LAVORTER

I had brought a *Sacher Torte*, the famous classic Viennese cake to the next session, to celebrate the one-year anniversary of Peter finishing his last drink. We'd agreed that this time he would bring his wife Laura to do a round-up of what this first year without alcohol had meant to them as a couple.

When they entered my therapy room, I could sense a tension in the air which would not be undone any-time soon by any chocolate delicacy, with or without whipped cream. When the four of us were seated, I tried to break ground.

"Laura, so nice to finally meet you. I feel I know you from the many talks with Peter, but it's great to see you in person. Let me start by congratulating you both because it's as much your anniversary as it is Peter's. We tend to forget how hard recovery is also on the partner."

"Well, thank you, Dr. Lavorter. Yes, for sure this past year has not been a walk in the park, but I'm encouraged that, from here on, things will get better." Laura's tone of voice was sociable yet formal at the same time. Her poise and appearance made it clear that we were dealing with a confident woman who was used to running her own show. Impeccably dressed in Burberry's, she had an air of sophistication about her. The way she handled herself gave a clear message that she had her own agenda and that she was not Peter's plus-one at any party.

Seeing her up close, I could now perfectly picture how her ultimatum had been the final catalyst for Peter to give up the booze. She was a striking woman as well as a sharp cookie. I felt that establishing trust with Laura would be critical in getting to the next stage. It wouldn't be the first time that the partner of a recovering addict would regard the therapist as an intruder, interfering in a private situation between husband and wife. I would need to understand where she was coming from, get into her head, so to speak.

"Please do call me 'Catherine,'" I said.

She acknowledged my invitation with an understated smile, as if she would rather stay on a last-name basis. I instantly knew this wasn't going to be easy. It made me wish I'd prepared better for this encounter. I decided to play the medical card first.

"There's a reason why making it to one year sober is a big milestone. Twelve months without drinking go a long way in dealing with the inevitable post-acute withdrawal symptoms like mood swings and angst. It's a scientific fact that the mind needs much more time to kick the habit than the body does. Over the past year, Peter's brain has been able to repair most of the psychological damage inflicted by years of alcohol abuse."

Laura did not waste any time. "So when will Peter be better, in your opinion?"

I hesitated just a fraction of a second, long enough to imply that there was no simple answer to this question. "His anxiety levels have finally started to diminish, and he has a more positive outlook on life. That is what I've observed these last couple of sessions. But there are still issues he has to work through."

I could see that Peter was hesitating to say something. I waited for a minute but then continued, in order to give him more time to prepare a reaction. "Recovery from substance abuse is all about dealing with the past and learning how to live a self-directed life without alcohol or drugs. It takes time." I was aware that I was using jargon to keep Laura at arm's length. Her direct communication style had me somewhat bewildered and on the defensive. But she was relentless.

"Yeah, well, I know it's been hard for him this past year, but now I need my husband back. I know he's in there somewhere." She briefly smiled at her own joke but then quickly regained her serious composure.

"I'm sure you feel that way," I said. "But please know that Peter has been crossing an emotional minefield. He is trying to make it safely to the other end, but he's not there yet."

I now looked Peter straight in the eye, as I wanted him to speak up. And he did.

"You know, Doc, in the past weeks, leading up to this one-year mark, I was actually nervous. As if part of me could still not believe I was actually going to make it to a full year without a single drink." With this statement, he did not exactly address his wife's plea for a return to normalcy. They seemed to be on different tracks, and I could see this clearly frustrated her.

I decided to follow his track. "Anniversary anxiety is very normal in early recovery, Peter. Don't you worry. The familiar voice of addiction rose to the occasion once again and made a final attempt to be heard. I can imagine that it suggested that you were too weak to make it to one year sober, that you might as well give up and not embarrass yourself further, correct?"

Peter nodded while Laura was looking for something in her purse, which was very distracting. I gathered my thoughts and focused on Peter.

"Maybe it whispered that there's really no point to all your hard work, because in the final analysis you will drink again. Sound familiar?" I asked.

"Yes, yes, and yes."

He sounded relieved that I seemed to know what had been going through his head.

"But every day that passes makes you stronger. Of course, you still notice the cravings, but you do not give in to them. At times, you are tempted, yet you consciously do not respond to temptation. This non-reacting is in fact what is strengthening your sobriety by wearing down your escapist tendencies. You are showing yourself how to do it . . . by doing it."

I looked first at Peter and then at Laura. "So to sum up, today is not just another day. It is a special day, as the wheel of time has made one full revolution with Peter staying sober."

Peter clearly appreciated the praise, while Laura looked at me skeptically. I could read on her face that she was wondering what made one year so damn special. "Alright, let me briefly explain what I mean here. Today one year ago was also a sober day for Peter, while the day before was still a drinking day. This one day makes all the difference in the world."

Laura's expression was still the same. "It may sound like superstition, but many of my patients tell me that they were on more solid ground after a full three-hundred-and-sixty-five-days on the wagon. It meant they had come full circle, rubber-stamping their recovery. It made it more official, somehow."

As I expected, Laura had a comment. "But surely a year is just a psychological milestone. It's not a scientific landmark?"

"Time keeps turning ad infinitum," I said, "and to cut it down to human size we've divided it up on the basis of what we see in nature. The one-year cycle represents the most universally relevant interval we know. From spring over summer, to autumn and finally winter."

I could see Laura got my point now. And Peter seemed to find inspiration in this.

"I completely orbited the sun without a drink." He had been staring into space, but now he was focused. "You know, it does feel like I've passed an important test. I can now face other recovering alcoholics with more legitimacy. I don't have to brace every time I see people drinking because I've started to trust myself again. It feels like I'm finally getting my life back."

Hearing Peter say these words out loud, Laura's demeanor seemed to turn 180 degrees. Her face lit up, as she was clearly taking energy from any positive sign that he was able to give her. She must have been really starved for any proof of life from him after such a long period of relapse and recovery. I instantly felt guilty for having judged her so harshly earlier.

Laura, Adaline, and I were now looking at Peter in the way that proud parents beam over their six-year-old's first report card in a parent-teacher conference.

After a minute, I noticed that all this attention made Peter acutely self-conscious. His wife's presence here today clearly brought a very different dynamic to the session. He seemed less sure of himself, nervous about her reactions.

While I was considering how to proceed, I observed from the corner of my eye how Laura took a moment to appraise Adaline in a way that only women do with each other. It made me glance sideways at my bright, young therapist, and suddenly I saw her through Laura's eyes. Adaline Vikander's Nordic heritage clearly shows in the elegant nose, the full cheeks with the impossibly high cheekbones and the captivating smile. That face, together with the tall, model-like figure makes the total package kind of intimidating. Adaline is a powerful affirmation of the stereotyping that has Scandinavian ladies consistently in the number-one position in the most attractive women polls. Come to think of it, her face is ridiculously perfect. It must be a ten on the golden ratio scale, the so-called divine proportion, which men find irresistibly appealing.

I can't help but think of the many occasions when my male patients were simply wonderstruck whenever she entered the room. The first minutes of a session were usually about getting them back down to earth. It's a known fact that a man's perception of female beauty is hardwired into his being. It turns him powerless because he simply has no defense against this subconscious attraction. And Peter is a bit of a ladies' man, anyway, although he would probably never admit it.

In short, Adaline is completely enthralling and dazzling to the male eye and, in stark contrast, a predatory mantrap to the female observer. And for sure, I could see Laura scanning Adaline's icy-blue eyes, the full lips, the white-blond hair done up in a playful ponytail. And then down to the long legs, the high heels, and the grey pencil skirt riding up just a bit too high above the knee. All the while, Adaline was just sitting in her chair, innocently taking notes. Then Laura's gaze finally landed upon poor Peter, who also happened to be looking at Adaline. A most unfortunate timing.

I had a strong sense that Laura did not appreciate the fact that Peter had omitted telling her that one of his co-therapists was, in fact, this stunning young woman sitting here in all her glory. That is, if he had mentioned Adaline at all in his accounts to Laura. I could see a million questions in Laura's eyes, but I was confident that she would use her emotional intelligence when confronting her husband after the session, which I was sure she would do.

And it was only normal for Laura to feel protective of Peter, now that she finally had him back. They had battled side by side against the addiction. She was not about to give him any room now to even look at an attractive woman, especially one with a striking resemblance to Blake Lively.

As a side-note here, I've only come to know that Adaline looks anything like Blake Lively, the sexy Californian actress, because my own husband happened to mention this to me, after a function we attended together with Adaline at Geneva University. Which reminds me that I still need to ask him how he knows of Blake Lively, anyway. Men!

Adaline looked up from her yellow notepad and spoke in a tone that could not hide her impatience after what she no doubt considered to be small talk. "Peter, I found it striking that your state of mind in Bangalore was the complete opposite of that in Bangkok. You were focused and in the present in India, compared with the ego-craziness in Thailand."

Peter was tuned in to the fact that something had been going on between the women, but he was clueless as to what it could be. He looked very relieved at the chance to answer an actual question and jumped on this passing train.

"Yeah, that's right. I love traveling in India. It's one of the few places where I can stay in the now without much effort. I do wonder what it is about India that prevents the mind from wandering."

Now that we were on topic, I, too, had a couple of things to say about his latest writing. "I found it quite ironic how you had that memorable conversation with the old man about the fact that time is only a construct of the mind while the very structure of your story was a memory flashback."

"Glad you noticed, Doc." He smiled at me, pleased that the built-in paradox had not escaped me.

I wanted to say more, but before I had a chance, Adaline jumped back in. "That ending was brutal, though. Your lovely descriptions of the wedding prepa-rations and the ceremony quite frankly had me on cloud nine. Then, to learn that Anika was beaten to death by extremists was a total upset." She gave him a look that was both stern and affectionate and added, "You either have a great imagination, or you are a true magnet for life-or-death situations."

"I'm afraid the story was true. Laura and I attended Anika's Hindu funeral in Bangalore, five days after I got the voicemail from the police commissioner. Both families were there, as well as a great many sympathiz-ers. Frankly, it was hard to watch."

Laura nodded affirmatively, thereby wiping away all doubts. This frankly surprised me, as I had been convinced the story's ending had been fiction, rather than fact.

And then Laura took the lead again. "I wonder whether we could talk now about how Peter and I can resume a more normal life. I feel he's still living in the past, what with all the stories and the psychoanalysis. I would like us to get back into the flow of things."

Her assertive statement alarmed me. It dawned on me that Laura was here not so much to take stock of the past year but to get Peter to face forward rather than backward. She wanted us to throw him a jolt. Without a doubt, this would change his perspective, but I could see also how it could put immense pressure on him.

"I understand the way forward is very important to you. You have been extremely patient with Peter. You've supported him through years of heavy drinking, four stints of rehab, and three relapses. And the past year of sobriety can't have been easy, with the heavy withdrawal symptoms and the melancholic state of mind. I am appreciative of all this, but—"

Laura was not to be placated, and she interrupted me without hesitation. "Look, Dr, Lavorter, I am still supportive of the therapy. It's just that I want it now to take on a new direction. Peter has to take his destiny in his own hands. Let the past be the past—it's time to move on."

It was obvious that the couple had discussed all of this at home before the session, because Peter now fell

223

seamlessly in line with his wife, clearly eager to sustain the new momentum in their relationship. "Doc, Laura is right. I want you to help me enjoy the present. I have been reading up on meditation and mindfulness lately, and I would like our next sessions to focus on those techniques. When I was much younger, I could really find joy in being completely focused in the here and now. Well, I would like to get to that happy place again. Be in the zone and all that."

I was actually glad they seemed to agree on this.

"You both referred just now to getting back into the flow, into the zone. I want to take this literally for a moment. Peter, can you recall a situation in which you were fully immersed in what you were doing without the need to think? No room in your mind for conflict or contradiction, just peace? 'Flow' means different things to different people, and I want to make sure I understand what it represents to you."

Peter took a moment to gather his thoughts.

"Well, what comes to mind is a wonderful episode in Amsterdam, early on in my career, when I really thought that my ship had come in. I was part of a great team then, and we were convinced we were about to get very rich. We were in sync with the laws of the universe, so to speak. Everyone was doing the best they could, and everything we touched seemed to turn into gold." He stopped for a moment and looked out the window, savoring the memory. "I can still feel the excitement now. There was a sense of belonging, a feeling of connectedness. Nothing could stop us."

Adaline did not waste any time. "That is flow, all right! I'd love to read about that time in Amsterdam, Peter."

I smiled at her and nodded my agreement to him. "Yes, I agree it's a good idea for you to write about that experience so we can leverage it as a model for future flow experiences."

Then I looked up at the clock. "Peter and Laura, I'd like to use our remaining time today to briefly touch upon mindfulness as a concept. I do believe that it makes sense for Peter to try to live more fully in the present moment. To master this is to accept and not resist the facts as they are." Then I faced Peter again. "Your dialogue in India with the old man was telling. You stated you're not ready to accept things as they are—you still constantly want to change the world and yourself to fit your own expectations."

Peter nodded cautiously.

"Being mindful means that you willingly stop the tyranny of your mind. Face the fact that often things will not work out the way your mind wants them to and that your personal preferences only cause frustration and resistance. Therefore stop identifying with your mind."

Laura was quick to confirm my words.

"I strongly agree with that, Dr. Lavorter." She quickly corrected herself. "'Catherine,' I mean."

I briefly smiled and nodded her to go on.

"I feel we're never really together in the moment," she said. "Peter's always regretting his years of drinking, the time lost and all the opportunities missed. And he's constantly worrying of what will come next. All of that does not help us to move forward, not one inch."

Peter's pained expression revealed that he was torn between a firmly defensive reaction and a willingness to discuss what had just been put on the table. He decided to play along and not fight his wife on this. "Well, it's true that I still get frustrated with things, and I know that just accepting them as they are would make things easier. Rather than trying to change my world, I should try to change my attitude toward it, right?"

All three of us nodded, and Adaline said, "Peter, I believe you need to take some risk and re-engage with life, but in a mindful manner. You should move forward with a new project, even if you do not have guarantees that things will always work out the way you'd like them to. I think you'd find this new mindset liberating and exciting. Life is fun, and what you need is a new challenge to bring your A-game to the table once again."

Adaline had a knack for saying the right thing at the right time. It was unfortunate that our time together had run out for today.

Laura had the last word on the matter. "That's exactly what I have been suggesting all along—let us start something new together. We can go for a trip around the world or do some serious volunteering work in a faraway place. Let's jump in without overthinking it. I, for one, am ready."

With this urgent invitation now very much out in the open, the couple left the therapy room. Laura seemed very happy with the way that the session had ended. But I could not help but wonder whether Peter felt ambushed and overpowered by three women who seemed to be in full agreement about what he should do next.

CHAPTER 22

PRISM

BY PETER BAER

I still recall that long, hot August day in the summer of 2000 like it was yesterday.

"Never Be the Same Again," by English singer-songwriter Melanie C is blasting from the sound system. The music carries over the water, reverberates against the high cement walls of the Prinsengracht and then farther down Amsterdam's concentric canal belt. With broad smiles on our faces, we raise our champagne flutes in a toast to a fabulous start to the new millenium. The sun shines like a diamond, and we feel like masters of the universe.

What we are is a team of young expats, gathered on the deck of an Amsterdam canal cruise ship, celebrating the success of our fledgling start-up company. Our

CEO Brent, a Canadian serial entrepreneur, calls for attention. "Team, here's to us making it big! Cheers!"

At that exact moment, behind him and high up on the quayside, two bike-riders collide into each other in a very silly way, distracted by our noisy celebration. We all burst out laughing, leaving Brent totally confused in the center, staring at us and wondering what's so funny. Wenke, the stunning redhead who is our HR manager, puts Brent out of his misery by sweetly whispering in his ear what just happened behind his back. As Brent's face clears up, we all laugh again and salute him, with glasses held up high.

A little over two years ago, this team spontaneously clustered together here in Amsterdam. From the very first day, the all-is-possible aura of this vibrant city had us totally psyched. It's not a fluke that this place has become Europe's number-one hotspot for Internet start-ups. The mood in this city is pregnant with energy.

In the past two years, we've worked our asses off. And we have not looked back once. At least not until today, gathered here on the water to celebrate our amazing success. We have plenty of reasons to be proud, since we have managed to position ourselves exactly in the right place at the right time to kick-start the Internet miracle on the old continent.

We followed the smart money from the States into Europe and became prime movers in the space of broadband infrastructure. We put glass fiber into the ground at an accelerating pace, trying to keep up with the market's insatiable appetite for high-speed bandwidth. And then we got noticed by Sequoia Capital, the early-stage venture capitalists who injected us with mountains of cash to keep us growing and eventually got us listed on NASDAQ, the stock exchange for high-risk dot-coms.

And that brings us to today.

Each of us here is now the proud owner of a ridiculous amount of stock options, the value of which runs into the millions. Our stock does not go up and down like normal stocks do. No, it only moves up, pushing our call options ever deeper in-the-money. Every morning as I wake up, I see that the price has gone up.

Every. Single. Day.

What this means is that literally each and every one of us, from the CEO all the way down to the receptionist, is now a dollar millionaire. At least on paper, that is. That is the angle. Our options do not vest for another eighteen months, so for now, we cannot cash in. We just have to sit tight and wait. But boy, does it feel good to be rich.

I am not too worried. Surely, this fortune cannot slip away from us, not when we have such forward momentum. No need to break our heads over something we cannot control, right?

I look around me and try to savor the moment. The wonderful Amsterdam canal district enjoys UNESCO

World Heritage status, and it sure is the perfect setting to our little party here today. The façades of the historic canal houses bear witness to the city's enrichment through maritime trade in the 17th century. This very city was the capital of the world economy in its day, and, as such, it is a venue fit for kings and queens and their contemporary equivalents. Yet, why do I feel out of place somehow?

The afternoon sun burns down heavily on the water, which de facto acts as a prism, breaking the sun's spectrum into its constituent colors. The sun's glitter is totally blinding, and there is something slightly disorienting about the way the white light is dispersed into its basic colors. Especially the violet and blue hues somehow give these historic settings a sinister look and feel. I wonder whether the others here feel the same way or it's just me. I realize I'm stuck in my head again, and I force myself to come back to the here and now.

I look at my fellow entrepreneurs. The girls are wearing short, flowery summer dresses and have their hair done in a sleek blowout. They sure look lovely and full of life. The men wear geek t-shirts with the unavoidable tongue-in-cheek, nerdy quotes such as "Life would be much easier if I had the source code" and "I can explain it to you but I can't understand it for you." We're quite the assorted group: Irish, Dutch, North-American, French, Belgian, and two Belarussian network engineers who only speak Internet Protocol.

If not by language, we're connected through our skills and passion for the Internet. We are wired in and fully engaged in our craft.

I zoom in on one young woman in particular. I'm not the only one who finds it difficult to take his eyes off Natasha. She's our PR lady, and, from the start, she's been the face and voice of our little company. Tash is a true beauty, resembling a young Charlize Theron, her fellow South-African. Like Theron, she has perfect skin, flame-gold hair, jade-green eyes, and the smile of a movie star. And to make her truly irresistible, she wears cherry-red lipstick.

Tash grew up in the affluent suburbs of Pretoria, at the height of Apartheid. She wanted a taste of the freedom and equality that Europe had to offer, and so she eventually made it over to Amsterdam, the city where anything goes. When she and Brent met one summer evening two years ago in a bar on Rembrandt Square, they hit it off over drinks and simply agreed for Tash to become the start-up's public relations manager. Right away, her natural enthusiasm spilled over into the job. Tash has been simply brilliant at putting us on the map with her off-the-wall approach to advertising.

Along with the other young men here, I've had a secret crush on Tash since the very first time I saw her. The fact that we all know that Tash has a lover back home in Pretoria, a guy she rarely speaks about, just adds to her mystery.

Our Operations Director, Tony, is from Nebraska, and I observe how he and Tash are standing at the very front of the ship, deep into a heated discussion on driving Lexus versus Porsche, happily spending money they do not have yet. I can't help but smile. Our future sure looks lavish with opportunity. The prospect of getting filthy rich is wildly appealing and brings with it the promise of complete freedom and autonomy. The thought of never having to work for a boss again, and being financially independent at a ridiculously young age, is as blinding as the sunlight is on the water.

Instinctively, I know that our success comes from the fact that as a team, we have achieved flow. We're at the top of our game, at the exact point of the curve where the challenge at hand matches the peak of our skills. The unrestrained energy we demonstrate every day comes from feeling unhindered by life's usual limitations. All the ordinary, everyday stuff is adjourned until we get to the end of this ride, for better or for worse. We have placed a big bet in life, and we're all in this together. It's like nothing I have experienced before. Even describing it can only come from the gut—my mind doesn't seem to have access to the right vocabulary.

Our motivation is intrinsic, and our focus is contagious. The company's hierarchy is symbolic because each of us inherently knows what to do. Our game plan is intuitive. Our marketing tagline is "Failsafe." That is how confident we are. Each of us is a domain expert and as a team, we shoot for zero errors.

In our office, we've named our conference rooms after famous prison complexes, like Sing Sing, Alcatraz, and Robben Island, in order to remind ourselves not to waste precious time in there. Staying in the zone is key to our survival, and meetings are like poison.

We feel privileged because stars and planets have aligned for something this extraordinary to happen. We come as close to feeling immortal as we ever will. And yet, deep down I know something is very wrong.

Staring down at the waterline, the word "prism" lingers from my earlier thoughts about the sunlight refracting in the canal water. When light travels from air into water, it slows down and changes direction slightly, like a prism. Ever since I was a small child, I have understood that you cannot see straight through a prism because it bends the light.

I feel annoyed with myself. Why can I not simply enjoy this beautiful afternoon? My mind sure has a way of screwing up memorable moments like this, with its constant, irrelevant background drivel. But then I mentally see the metaphor. It's telling me that maybe I'm blind to what is right in front of me.

The elated mood we've been in as a group and the exciting thoughts about unlimited wealth have acted like a prism, bending our reality. If something seems too good to be true, it probably is.

I realize that our small company is years away from turning a profit, yet our stock price is sky high, based upon unrealistic market expectations and a great deal of emotion surrounding the Internet boom. What if this is just an illusion, a castle in the air?

If I could run to the bank right now and cash in on my options at fifty cents on the dollar, I would not hesitate one minute. But the option's vesting schedule has me in a golden cage, and that's a pain. So I've really got no choice but to believe the bubble will not burst.

I tell myself that I'm in this to the very end. After all, the analysts are falling over themselves to convince the public that this is only the start of the boom cycle. I'd be crazy not to sail the strong tailwind of the new economy and miss out on the gold rush. I just need to remind myself every day to stay bullish. Right?

The sun disappears behind the roofs of the historic buildings. The temperature takes a sudden drop, and I see that the girls are putting on jackets and sweaters. The last thing I remember from that day is that I almost physically brush my worries away. I raise my glass for a refill, and the ever-present alcohol somewhat keeps me in my precious but delicate bubble. But there's no denying that my earlier lightheartedness has gone for good, as if while floating on the water, unknowingly, the ship has passed a tipping point.

With perfect hindsight, that day in Amsterdam was a defining moment. The dot-com collapse that soon followed turned our stock options into worthless paper as the new economy crashed and burned in a spectacular fashion. Giddy investors suddenly sobered up after figuring out that web businesses with little revenue and no profit were fundamentally worthless. A global recession kicked in, and the 2000 crash will be remembered forever as the speculative bubble that wiped out five trillion dollars of stock market value.

This was also the end to our dream team. When the prospects of great wealth evaporated, we each went our own way, looking for new horizons. We said our goodbyes and swore friendships for life, but at the same time, we were sure that this would not reproduce itself. Not in a million years. Stars and planets had already drifted back into their normal orbits. The magic spell had ended.

Looking back now, we were very lucky coming out with only our egos bruised. But in that very moment, it felt as if our universe had imploded on us and we were reduced again to being mere mortals.

I did not get rich there and then, but I did take a couple of priceless things with me from that afternoon. Of course, there was that bittersweet flavor of immortality, right there on the water. Looking through that prism, we were the quintessential circle of young people celebrating existence and signing up for eternal youth, convinced we had discovered the elixir of life.

And then there was that remarkable feeling of flow, leading to absolute peak experience when all ego fell away, and our actions and thoughts became automatic. Our focus had completely absorbed us and had left us without a sense of time but with limitless opportunity. At the time, I had enough sense to capture and bottle that precious feeling of flow because I knew I would need it someday.

And now, one year sober, I have a burning need to drink from this elixir in order to bring myself back to life.

CHAPTER 23

CACHE

BY CATHERINE LAVORTER

I did not take my usual seat but rather invited Adaline to sit directly opposite Peter, which she did without hesitation. I saw this took him by surprise.

"As you can see Peter, our arrangement is a bit different today. I am putting Adaline in charge of this session. I have asked her to summarize our work up to now and confront you with a set of defunct perspectives on your part that we believe causes continued ambivalence in your thinking. I reviewed the material upfront, of course."

Peter looked at Adaline as if he were seeing her for the very first time. As usual, he was flustered by her apparent star quality, and it would take him a couple of minutes to pick himself up from the floor.

"This is as much to your benefit as it is to hers. As you know, Adaline is doing her internship here, and this is part of her final assignment. I trust this is okay with you?"

Peter, still processing the new set-up, quickly nodded his approval. After this brief opening statement, I was determined to keep my silence for the entire session. "Adaline, the floor is yours."

Adaline held her yellow notepad in her lap, obviously well-prepared for the occasion. "What I would like to do today is to address some of your old beliefs and to check whether we have been successful in opening up your mind to new ways of looking at them. Is that okay?" she asked.

"Sure. What exactly do you mean with 'old beliefs'?"

"Scripts which are clearly obsolete, yet you feel you have no choice but to follow them to the letter. Old tape recordings that are no longer relevant but still play over and over in your mind and keep triggering the same worn-out, unhelpful reactions. In short, imperfect thoughts is what I'm talking about."

He looked puzzled, but she continued unfazed. "Let's jump right in—it will all be clear in a moment." She stood up and walked briskly toward a flip chart in the corner of my office. She went ahead and uncovered a page with six bullets of text written in her neat, girlish handwriting:

- I am a separate, isolated individual in a random, brutal cosmos.
- I will die, therefore, I am doomed.
- I cannot make it on my own.
- I am my mind. I am my fears.
- I need to control everything in my life. I have no access to a higher power.
- I cannot be happy.

It was painful to watch the expression on Peter's face while he was reading the bullets in silence. He looked absolutely shell-shocked when he realized that, from a long series of therapy sessions, all of his sealed-up misery was being cruelly and unceremoniously summarized and exposed here on one single page, and by Adaline, no less.

If necessary, I was ready to speak up and defend Adaline's idea to discuss all of these misconceptions all in one go. We'd both felt we had to tackle these lingering twists of his mind until none of them would be left standing.

The human psyche comes configured with a cache, a space needed to store our darkest fears, shame, and guilt. For people like Peter, who have been drinking for many years exactly not to have to face that subconscious hiding place, it sure was an alien experience to see these unexamined impulses suddenly disclosed on a sheet of paper. Clearing that cache in Peter's mind of its toxic content was the only way to finally stop his anxiety from overflowing into his daily functioning. He told us a few sessions ago that he wanted to drain the abscess. Well, this was it.

Adaline did not give him time to protest or question the approach. "What I want to do today is to address each statement and make a strong case for its exact opposite. Then I want to check with you whether the original phrase as it's written here still holds true for you, or we can file it away as no longer valid."

He nodded that he understood, yet he looked like he'd rather be anywhere else but here.

"I want you to be completely honest and open, alright?" she said. "This is a safe place, and you can trust me."

Peter was about to say something, but instead he swallowed hard. His body language expressed the profound dilemma he found himself in. Instinctively, he wanted to stop this whole thing right in its tracks, and, at the same time, he just knew he had to let go of his reservations and follow Adaline's lead. In a tone that held the middle between sarcasm and resignation, he responded. "This should be interesting; please go on."

I could see that he was highly strung and extremely focused. Any other mindset would have come as a surprise, as Adaline had spent hours going over the hundreds of pages of therapy notes to distill these six emotionally charged assertions that Peter had made at some point during treatment. To him, this went right to his heart. We had just turned up the voltage of controversy to the maximum.

I took a moment to look at my student. Adaline's performance so far had been flawless, as far as I was concerned. She seemed once more very sure of herself today. She was dressed in an elegant two-piece suit that was neither provocative nor revealing. The unavoidable high heels were the only reminder of her former ensembles. I surely approved of her recent style upgrade. It made me wonder whether at some level she had become aware she could get barred from graduation over dress code. Silly thought. As if I would let that influence my opinion of her.

"Let's get started then," she said.

Adaline used a laser pointer to highlight the first bullet while reading the phrase out loud. The red laser beam gyrated around the words like a sniper would fix his mark in the crosshairs of his riffle scope, while calibrating for distance and wind speed.

"I am a separate, isolated individual in a random, brutal cosmos."

She paused for effect while striking a power pose, standing tall with her feet apart, hands on her hips and chin tilted slightly upward. Her blond pony-tail took a few seconds to stop swishing.

I was fairly sure she was deploying this self-assured look in order to make Peter respond in kind with the same confidence. It did not have the intended effect, however, as I watched him touching his neck, a gesture well-known to suggest a lack of control and a general state of anxiety.

I felt for him while Adaline moved swiftly onwards.

"Peter, you covered this very topic of isolation in a very poignant way in your story 'Angst' when you found yourself swimming away from shore to the point of almost drowning in the Caribbean Sea. You said you felt unobserved and left to your own devices without a higher power looking out for you."

Peter, now fully vigilant, responded instantly. "Very true—it still gives me the shivers to think of that episode. I will always remember that moment in the ocean as a harsh confrontation with the absolute absurdity of existence. It hit me that there was nobody who could give meaning to my life but me."

"Yes, and that conclusion was the correct one, as only you are the creator of your own experience," she said.

This angle was new to him.

"What I mean is, Peter, for all practical purposes, perception is reality. You take the world into yourself with your senses, and you color it with your mind. And that coloring affects your actions and reflects back out to the world. It's a two-way street, and, in that sense, you are not isolated. You give your world a unique flavor, and it throws that flavor right back at you."

He looked at her doubtfully.

"Clear and simple," she continued. "If you are afraid, then everything will look scary. If you have a positive outlook, however, then the world will smile right back at you."

"I am not so sure of that," he said. "I feel I have precious little impact on my world. If only I could better understand its cardinal logic, then at least it could all start to make sense to me. Then I would be able to cooperate with it, like I do in business life."

Adaline was smiling as if she had maneuvered Peter exactly into the position where she wanted him. She spoke in a soft, sweet voice, as if gently correcting the skewed logic of a child. "The operating principles of the universe do not need your cooperation, Peter. The same inescapable laws continue to support your life even if you do not acknowledge them." She had his full attention with this counterintuitive claim. "But here's the thing, Peter: In order to feel safe and connected, rather than threatened and isolated, it helps if you align with the foundations of life rather than fight them."

This triggered a definite irate reaction on his part. "But be specific—align with what? That is exactly my problem. I do not see any foundations to align with. If there would be a fucking Ikea manual to life, I think I would have read it by now."

Adaline ignored his outburst, coolly leaning over my desk, thumbing through her notes, looking for a particular page in her thick notepad. When she had found it, she looked up at him, keeping her finger fixed on a particular spot.

"Well, you did it at least once before—align with life, that is. On that boat in Amsterdam, you said you felt a wonderful connectedness with others, you said you achieved flow with your team, you were right there in the moment and in sync with the laws of the universe. You said that stars and planets aligned, that you were in the right place at the right time, that you intuitively knew what to do and that the possibilities seemed limitless."

I thought she was borderline arrogant now, and I wondered whether she would get away with it. To top it off, she said, "Your words."

"Yeah, so?" he responded, still sounding angry.

"It means that deep down, you know very well how to follow the river of life," she said. "You even made a closing remark in your Amsterdam story that you were glad to have captured and bottled that feeling for later use. Unknowingly, you were sending a message to your future self."

There was a brief pause.

"Peter, you need to drink now from the elixir you discovered back then."

He only just now seemed to fully recall the punch line of his recent "Prism" narrative of the events on the Amsterdam canals and probably wondered why he had blocked this out of his memory. Adaline was driving her point home.

"Peter, I believe you do realize that life has the ability to run itself," she said.

"Run itself?"

"Yes, that there is a central intelligence that drives things forward. Everything is not just coincidence, nor can it be controlled by human intervention. The universe has its own rules that have governed it for billions of years, long before man existed. It does not need your blessing or your pitiful efforts to steer it in the direction of your personal preferences. The only thing that does is to create frustration on your part."

Although Peter seemed to resent being lectured like this, I could see that basically he got the gist of what Adaline was saying. "I am willing to accept that. But what is the lesson here?"

"That you can decide to relax and feel more at home in this world, by accepting the idea that you are cared for. That you can afford to let life unfold because it is not your enemy. That you are part of a grander scheme."

"I am cared for?" He sounded incredulous.

"Yes, you should trust that you are protected by an invisible factor that is preserving life through all its apparent chaos. Random events are not random but form intelligent patterns. Cause and effect is one such pattern."

I saw a spark in Peter's eye, a sign of recognition. He was on familiar territory now. "Cause and effect."

"Yes. Actions have consequences. What goes around comes around. Karma." She spoke matter-of-factly.

Emboldened, he answered. "Now that is one concept I understand well."

"Yes, you understand it well but only in the corporate domain of buying and selling. Cause and effect in the shape of cold transactions aimed at making a profit. What I am talking about here is the altruistic version of that."

"Ah. I see." His tone slightly sarcastic again.

"This is hardly new to you, Peter. You earlier described the domino effect of doing good in your story 'Ether,' about the dying girl donating her organs so others could live. Causing a rippling effect throughout Singapore, expanding like concentric circles in a pond. Michelle's example proving a real inspiration to many others."

"Are you saying I should aim for the greater good and, automatically, good stuff will start to happen to me? Cosmic karma will reward me for my positive actions?"

She spoke in a whisper now, with great deference to a concept that she obviously believed in deeply. "Yes, Peter, that is exactly what I mean. Stop being cynical, because that is not who you really are. Open yourself up to life, and it will treat you well. Whatever you do will always come back to you. Surely you have heard of the golden rule that says to treat others the way you would like to be treated?"

Suddenly humbled, Peter responded: "Sure I have."

"Well, it seems to me that you have not yet taken that principle to heart, not even when you became sober. Even though you comprehend it well because you wrote about it in some brilliant ways. But now is the time to practice what you preach."

Peter took a deep breath, closed his eyes, and, much to my surprise, nodded affirmatively. "I get the message—thank you. This actually feels liberating. It hadn't occurred to me to leverage cause and effect as a ways to giving something back to the community, to engage myself at a deeper level. I have been too preoccupied still with my image of big-league business executive, I guess."

Adaline smiled, and, without further ado, her laser pointer moved swiftly to the second bullet on the flip chart. She was not one for wasting time.

"I will die, therefore, I am doomed."

Peter immediately reacted. "I'll be honest with you, seeing that up there hurts like hell. Remember when I told you that each morning I wake up to yet another day without a solution to my mortality problem?"

She nodded.

"Well, I wasn't kidding. That never-ending death terror feels like impending doom, I swear."

"Let me be crystal clear here. Your constantly being aware of your eventual demise has the potential benefit of making your life more salient, if you let it. Because you know it will end, you really have no choice but to make the most of it, at this very moment. Only by fully living in the present will you be able to look back at the very end and say that it was all worth it. And then go in peace, like your father showed you."

"But still, the very thought of death paralyzes me," he said.

"It will stop doing that, the exact moment that you let go of your self-importance. You are scared of death not for itself but because of an instinctive fear that your fragile ego will break down. Fragile because it is based upon money, status, and power, like we just discussed."

Peter looked at me and then back at Adaline. "I suddenly realize that I came to that very same conclusion in my Bangkok story 'Hubris,' right? That life was giving me a second chance, and I owed it to myself to take it with both hands, but also to change my ways. A man reborn."

Peter was still clueless to the fact that Adaline had cleverly based her list of bullets upon his very own writings. He was now referencing his own stories, thinking the correlation was completely coincidental. Both Adeline and I were doing our best to suppress a smile. Adaline was very convincing, while she continued.

"Exactly. The car crash in Bangkok stripped you from the illusion that you were invulnerable. Neither your business skills nor your ice-cold logic could protect you from that fatal road accident. Turns out you were not so special after all."

Peter was hanging on to her every word as she went on. "With that crash, you came to realize that you'd been living in bad faith for a long time and for all the wrong, ego-tripping reasons. And the fact that the little girl in the red dress was unharmed was a clear invitation to start over in life, sober and humbled. A wake-up call and a second chance at the same time. Not many people get that."

"So if I understand it correctly, all of our talk here today points me in the direction of a more modest way of living, one in which I do not put myself first all the time," he said.

"Yes. And that modest attitude will strengthen your self-esteem into something more solid and not just built on the quicksand of riches and standing. Then, with a stronger self-esteem, your death fear will diminish. And if you are no longer afraid to die, you will no longer be afraid to live. You will no longer feel doomed."

Peter let out a sigh of relief. He visibly relaxed, as if a heavy load had just lifted. Adaline looked at him for a long minute, and then she cast a furtive glance at me. I was about to suggest a coffee break, but before

I did, Adaline pointed to the third bullet on the flip chart. There was no stopping her.

"I cannot make it on my own," she read. "I want to point to a connection between what we just said and another one of your stories, 'Catharsis,' the one about your mother."

He looked at her questioningly, clearly unable to process all of this in real time. It would need to sink in.

"You were smothered and overprotected as a child by your mother, and you consequently suffered from abandonment fears throughout your childhood. You pointed out that it felt like you had used up your fair share of luck just by getting born and you would not be able to make it through life without your mother."

"It sounds weird when you put it that way," he said, "but yes, I guess that is correct. Where are you going with this?"

"I want to make you aware of your codependency on women throughout your life, also as an adult."

Peter listened, open-mouthed.

"I think your fear of abandonment did not stop when you reached adulthood. It seems to me that you attribute magical qualities to women, believing they can somehow provide sanctuary, like your mother did. I believe you are constantly afraid of losing their shielding, and, as such, I think you have an unhealthy reliance on women."

"Please do give me an example."

"Well, your drinking, for one. For the longest time, you could not quit the booze whatever you tried, but when Laura put that ultimatum on your plate, you did the impossible—you stopped drinking. You said, and I quote: 'She gave me a small miracle.'"

Peter was looking out of the window, lost in thought.

"Let me ask you," Adaline said. "Before you married Laura, was there ever a period when you were on your own, without a woman at your side?"

"Well, I've had my share of romances but only one serious relationship before I met Laura."

"Tell me about that, please."

"Claire was her name. We met when we were just nineteen, in our freshman year at Leuven University. I was love-struck by her, I really was. Head over heels. We were together for four years, on and off. The affair was a roller coaster. I was devoted to her, but she broke my heart. And then I broke hers. I really do not want to talk about it—it's too painful."

"I can imagine this is a tender subject, but indulge me. You said Claire broke your heart?"

"Yes, she cheated on me with a summer fling when she was vacationing with her parents in Spain."

"How did that feel?"

"Heartbreaking, I already said."

"Like deep betrayal?"

"Yes, I trusted her completely and her deceit took me completely by surprise. I was blindsided. It felt like a breach of faith."

"How did you find out?"

"When she came back from her vacation in Spain, we agreed to meet up. She'd told me nothing on the phone, just that she was back and she wanted to see me. I was so happy we'd be together again. I remember I had bought her a little necklace. When we finally met, she first kissed me, and, right after that, she confessed." He paused. "A Judas kiss, it now feels like. When she revealed the affair to me, my world just collapsed. I could not understand how she could do that. I thought she loved me. I felt like a fool, and the pain was simply unbearable."

"You trusted Claire like you trusted your mother not to leave you?" Adaline was relentless, and she stopped at nothing to make her point.

"Alright, I see what you are doing here. Claire and all the other women were just surrogates for my mother. Is that what you are implying?"

"We'll get to that," she said. "You say that the relationship with Claire was on and off. You mean at some point you forgave her for being unfaithful to you?"

"Yes, I did. I guess the relief of getting back together was stronger than the anger and the pain."

"Relief?"

"Yes, it felt like a lifeline had been restored."

His eyes got dreamy with nostalgia. He snapped out of it when Adaline said, "But you broke her heart, too?"

"Yes, a few weeks after Claire broke off with me, I met someone new. Her name was Elise. Claire could not believe how fast I got a new girlfriend. Of course, the affair with Elise ended when I got back together with Claire."

"Peter, sorry for being harsh. But it sounds like you made sure that, on the rebound, you found a replacement for Claire, and you used her to make Claire see what she was missing."

"You seem to be on a crusade here, Adaline. What do you want me to say?"

"Is it correct to say that, ever since you started seeing women, you have made sure there has never been an intermission, a time on your own?"

Peter had never given any thought to this. "I guess that is true, but I've always thought that just happened by accident, not by design."

"Do you now start to see there were deeper motives at work? You could not stand to be without a female partner, and you made damn sure there was an uninterrupted flow of women, each one a new chance for salvation. I am saying that you instinctively fell back upon the old belief that in no case should you get separated from your mother. Or her proxy."

"Although I get your point about codependency, you make it sound like I had dozens of partners, which is not the case, I can assure you. And I want to point out that I have been married to Laura for more than twenty years. The bond I have with her is not comparable to anything that came before. We are soul mates, and I love her."

"Point taken," Adaline said. "And yet I want to challenge this a bit further if you don't mind. Can you tell me what exactly it is about women that mesmerizes you?"

"'Mesmerize' seems like too strong a word, Adaline. You make it sound like I am under some kind of spell. I consider women to be more caring and attentive than men. And I admit that at times, I get overwhelmed by their charms. There is an undeniable magnetism to their loveliness. But I never act on that attraction." He looked like he wanted to say more, but he didn't.

"I believe that it would be good if you could lose the notion that somehow you need to woo women because you think they can save you."

Peter was clearly uncomfortable with this, but it was also obvious that Adaline had hit a nerve. It got him agitated. "But what makes you say this? What am I doing that would make you even think this?"

"I have seen how you look at me, Peter, and that's okay. I just want you to be aware of the deeper impulses that make you lose your normal powers of reason in the company of women. I believe you feel the need to pursue women in order to be protected by the mysterious powers you attribute to their beauty and charm. Again, like your mother protected you."

"I think you know you are lovely. It is only human that I look at you sometimes in an appreciative way. I apologize if I have offended you."

"No need to apologize, Peter. It's not about me personally. I just think you are unaware of how many girls feature in your stories, and how you glorify them."

He did exactly what Adaline expected him to do, which was to challenge her claim. "Well, why don't you give me some examples, then? Because I surely don't know what you're talking about."

Adaline proceeded to take a page out of her notes and started enumerating. "Well, let's see. There was the Russian girl in Vegas, Victoriya. Then we had Anika in Bangalore, Katya, the Ural girl in the elevator in Bangkok, Michelle in Singapore, and the South-African Natasha in Amsterdam."

Peter was turning red, but that, of course, did not stop Adaline.

"And let's not forget Conny, back in your very first story. Our patient zero, as Dr. Lavorter called her. I believe we now understand that Conny was the first proxy candidate. I remember you saying the rejection by Conny hurt so much because you realized you only had one life and you were never going to spend it with her. In other words, she was not going to be the one to save you."

Peter was silent.

"It's sweet really, this soft spot for the weaker sex that you have. I just wanted to point out what is obvious to the outside observer but probably not to you. Remember, looking through a prism will bend the reality of what is right in front of you."

She was being cocky now, while smiling her beautiful smile.

"I have a lot to digest. Can we call it a day?" It was plain to see that Peter was exhausted, which was fine, because the hour was up. And we did manage to cover half of the bullets.

CHAPTER 24

KERNEL

BY CATHERINE LAVORTER

We picked it up right were we left it, last time. Adaline pointed to bullet number four.

"I am my mind. I am my fears," she read. "Let me start with an analogy."

"Sure," Peter said. He looked well, great in fact. He had that sparkle in his eye today, like he was ready to move mountains.

"You know what wind chill factor is, right?" she asked. "The perceived lower temperature felt by your body due to the flow of air."

"Sure, I've experienced that particular circumstance many times on my trips to Russia. Winter time in windy St. Petersburg, close to the arctic circle, can feel like -30 C while in reality it is more like -15 C."

"Great, so you confirm that due to wind chill, the subjective, felt temperature can be much lower than the actual thermal reading of the air?"

"Yes, your point being?"

"Well, just like the wind adds iciness to the actual coldness, your thoughts and emotions add drama to reality. And that feels as real as the glacial wind on your skin. Your ego greatly exaggerates the importance of benign events. It tries to make life more exciting by adding frequently shifting storylines and intense feelings to the mix."

Peter was clearly amused by this unusual analogy. "Very clever. Wind chill."

"The ego-based world, with all its drama, is highly addictive, as you pointed out in your Vegas story 'Singularity.' The ego's agenda is to keep itself going. It needs a daily fix of theatricals and a constant denial that there is any escape from them."

"Yes, and we have already established that I have a supersized ego." His banter did not knock her off balance.

"Let me now refer to your 'Thousand Weddings' piece in Bangalore. You clearly heard the old man at the wedding say that you are the stillness at the bottom of the lake, not the ripples on the surface, right?"

"Sure thing," he responded.

"The crux of the matter is that there is an essential difference between you and your mind.

Your thoughts and emotions are just those evanescent wrinkles on the surface of the lake. Your fear is just the sub-zero wind that chills your face or a passing dark cloud that obscures the sun. But all the while, the real you lives above the fray. It is just the simplest version of you, unaffected by the mind. The kernel."

He was quick to catch on.

"That panic attack I had on the plane back from Mumbai, which seemed it was going to suffocate me, are you saying that was not real, it was just my mind playing tricks on me?" he asked.

"Exactly, that bout of panic was nothing but your repressed fears saying, 'Now that you are strapped in and vulnerable at forty-thousand feet in the air, I can make you look at me because you cannot escape.' Typical mind games."

"You know, I kind of get this, but how do I avoid my own mind ambushing me like that? I was able to eventually calm myself down on the plane, so I must be able to tap into hidden resources, even when my own mind is trying to sabotage my steady composure."

"We talked a lot about how you base your writing on intuition more than on thinking, right? You said it felt like someone was holding your hand. Dr. Lavorter called it your 'sixth sense.'"

"Yes, it's still a mystery to me how I do that, exactly."

"Well, we can demystify that one together, right here and now. While the mind agonizes over every angle of a situation, a deeper part of you knows already what to do. When writing, you tap into that pool of knowing, and the words spiral up. The challenge for you is to leverage that deeper instinct in everyday life and to bypass your mind."

"So you're saying that it's possible to actually stay in that peaceful state of mind and just ignore all bad thoughts and feelings?"

"The real you gets lost only when your mind starts identifying with thoughts such as 'I like this but not that. I am like this but not like that.' These ego-identifications quickly start leading their own life. The only way out is if you stop filtering life through the narrative of you and reach beyond your fake self."

"You remember from my discussion with the Indian guru that I have trouble doing exactly that." Peter was feeling uncertain, which usually translated into sarcastic statements like this one. Adaline looked down into her notes for a long minute.

"In the first weeks of therapy," she resumed, "when we were discussing your very first story 'Lovesick,' you said, and I quote: 'The story wrote itself, by letting a part of me take a step back and be a spectator to my thoughts and feelings.'"

"Yes, I remember that vividly. It felt like an out-of-body experience. Or better, an out-of-mind experience." He smiled faintly.

"Well, finding yourself is all about the 'Aha!' moment of discovering that second perspective, that of the silent witness, the watcher of all the thinking."

"I get a feeling of déjà vu here. My getting a phone call in that hotel room in Beijing from my sister telling me mother had died. Remember how I experienced a mental meltdown until everything stopped and I was reduced down to . . . well, down to a kernel. Just lying there in the dark on that hotel bed in China, no longer participating in any cerebral processes. Just this intense sense of familiarity, being again that five-year-old boy, walking in the snow at the hand of my mother."

"Yes. Your mind shut down out of self-preservation."

"Is that what we are talking about here?"

"Yes, but without the meltdown. This state can be induced voluntarily. Once you come to see that, at the level of the brain, everything is in flux, in a constant state of confusion, you can drift down to a lower stratum, where this confusion dissolves into stillness. Once you have found that place, you will want to live there."

"Is that where mindfulness comes in?" he asked.

"Yes, in fact mindfulness is all about observing the ego mechanism at work and relaxing into that second perspective we just discussed. If you can witness the thinking without getting wrapped up in it, you will find a deeper seat of awareness, one that is calm, alert, detached. Your center. I think we can now put this particular bullet point to bed, Peter. I believe you see now how you do not equal your mind. So don't believe everything it tells you. Shall we move on to the next one?"

Peter nodded, and Adaline pointed.

"I need to control everything in my life. I have no access to a higher power."

"On this one, you showed us the way forward with your ingenious Two PM on Everest sign post in the 'Tipping Point' narrative."

Adaline looked at me, and, despite the fact that I was going to keep quiet, I found myself saying, "Correct. Only in matters of life and death, like when you risk freezing to death on a mountaintop, is it paramount that you control the situation. Turning around and descending before two PM is a sensible way of doing that. But on days that you are not climbing Everest, metaphorically speaking, indeed you should just relax and let things unfold."

Adaline showed mild surprise that I was actually talking, so I quickly shut up. She took back the controls.

"To me this is the million-dollar question. You have shown you are great at making decisions, but can you also just let go? Can you accept this moment as it is?"

"Well, no. That much is clear," he said.

"And why do you think that is?"

"Because I always seem to be chasing something. I never think that now is enough; there is always something lacking."

"Exactly right. With addictive intensity, all these years you have been chasing too hard after money, thrills, work, and alcohol. Now, you are weary from all that chasing. And all this time, what you were looking for was right inside you."

"You mean I failed to find my center, like we just discussed?"

"Yes. Stop chasing worldly things because the world is messy," Adaline said. "The only thing that will ever be untainted is your own awareness once you sort it out. You have been focusing intently on your own grandiose drama all these years. Now you've come to understand that the outer world has no real power over you. Time to settle down and find your peace."

"I feel like I am trying very hard to do just that."

"Maybe you're trying too hard. Your mind is noisy now because you desperately try to control it. Like a wild horse, only when it is set free, the mind will settle down."

"You keep saying I should let go, I should set my mind free. But the whole thing feels like sand—the more I squeeze, the more it trickles through my fingers."

"Stop squeezing. Tactics that you have used successfully in business to get results will fail badly when you chase mindfulness. What you are looking for is already inside you. Let it unfold."

"So I have all the answers inside me?" This time, he did not try to hide his sarcasm.

"To anyone observing you, this is very obvious. This is what I meant when I said your tales tell me so much more about you then the formal therapy sessions. It is endearing to see how you are struggling to find external answers when they are so obviously stored inside you."

"This is frustrating, Adaline. I know you're right and yet, I do not know what it means in practice. What about that higher power? I see that many others find solace in their faith. It makes me furious that religion has eradicated that possibility for me. I can never again believe in God."

"Yes, that is one we need to tackle now. With pleasure, even." She took a sip of water and got going again. "You were indoctrinated by the dogma of the Catholic church as a boy. In therapy, you still often use words like *fallen* and *doomed*, which I believe are based upon that outdated religious script. The fall from grace, the being-thrown-from-Eden feelings you sometimes have is just a loss of who you really are, due to living in bad faith, untrue to yourself. You mix that genuine feeling with ancient biblical allegories about hell and condemnation. And I have the impression that you still suffer from that same childish misunderstanding of God."

"What do you mean exactly?" All of this seemed to make a big impression on Peter, like another box of Pandora was being opened. Or closed.

"Well, if there is such a thing as God," she said. "Then he is neither a person, nor a being, nor a spirit.

He is a power that includes all nature and the laws of nature. Like we said last time, these laws are neutral and equally true for everyone and everything. It is not God that takes care of us. We align with the laws of the universe, and we are supported."

"I see. So our discussion last time about leading a less self-centered life and giving something back—this is what you mean with 'alignment,' correct?"

"Yes. I strongly believe that you will undergo a spiritual transformation by doing that. And it will feel like a higher power will suddenly have a hand in your life. Be the best version of yourself, and the universe, like any mirror, will reflect back whatever you put in front of it."

Peter took a deep breath and looked relieved but shaky. Adaline said in a caring voice, "You okay?"

"This is heavy stuff. But good, very good."

"We're down to the last bullet. Are you up for it?" He nodded "Yes." As if he had a choice.

"I cannot be happy."

He looked at her like a puppy, eager to go for a long walk. These bullets were definitely growing on him.

"For the longest time, you thought sobriety and happiness were fully incompatible, didn't you?" she asked.

"Hell, yeah. The first six months were like a long, dark tunnel with no light at the end of it. Life sure did not seem worth living without alcohol."

"Funny that you happen to mention six months, because science tells us that is how long it takes to develop a new complex brain map. Your old neural pathways were deeply embedded in your brain due to the excessive drinking. It took you months and months of repeating the non-drinking version of every activity before it became a new habit. In the beginning, that sober pattern you were trying to weave was just too fragile to compete with the familiar drama of pain and pleasure that had you gripped for so many years, fueled by drinking. That clash makes for a very shitty feeling, to use a technical term."

Peter managed a smile. "True, especially when it came to doing things that I'd never done before without booze. Going to a restaurant, taking a vacation, winding down after a long day of stress on the job. The first time you try to do that in a sober state, it's almost ridiculous how lousy and unnatural it feels."

"And how do those things feel now?"

"Well, I'm not saying I enjoy them in the same way as I used to. I probably never will—it's just different. Once you accept that you will never drink again, then it actually becomes easier. When the internal fighting stops, there is a kind of surrender, and, with that, new things become possible. Slowly but surely, a new self-respect arises."

"You live life in a more intense way, right?" she said.

"Well, I still miss the thrill of drinking. But in its place came something much more relevant. For the first time ever, I'm actually examining my life and improving on myself. That is an incredible feeling. I think Dr. Lavorter called it 'life's paradox.' To find meaning despite the apparent absurdity. To remain positive despite the obvious fragility of it all."

He looked at me in appreciation, and, I must say, that was a welcome gesture. I decided I was going to contribute to this last bullet. I was sure Adaline would understand.

"Peter, it feels to me like you have made a crucial decision to let go of these old beliefs, these six bullets," I said. "With that, you're making a conscious decision to be happy. I don't know whether you realize that."

"Well, to be honest, I would not have guessed that these two last sessions could have such an impact. It was confrontational but liberating at the same time."

"Yes, I can see that. What you should absolutely retain is that you can relax into the rhythm of your own life and feel safe and at home, belonging, connected. Thoughts come and go, but you realize now that they are not reliable guides for what is real. Only the core of you is true."

Adaline looked at the clock and saw that our time was up. "Peter, there is a point of stillness within you around which everything revolves. You can live there, in that stillness. And I have a strong feeling you will."

CHAPTER 25

TEMPTATION

BY PETER BAER

I have been in Japan for the better part of a month now, and my flight back to Europe leaves at noon tomorrow. Finally. This will have been my last business trip to Asia before Laura and I start our sabbatical. We've taken the decision to both take a year off from work and spend it in India together.

First we will go to Pune, on the west coast of India, to spend three months at a Vipassanā meditation and yoga booth camp, run by a renowned Indian master teacher, then we move to Chennai in the southeast, where we will be volunteer helpers in a World Bank program that grants micro credits to local entrepreneurs to set up their own small businesses. They get modest amounts in the range of one hundred to one thousand dollars to start a small retail business to sell local products. Most importantly, they get a bank account and Internet access, which means they get connected to the world at large.

I am really looking forward to getting out of the rat race and actually reaching out to help other human beings. Apart from the fact that, to some extent, I am feeling liberated from my anxieties, this volunteering idea was the best thing that came from therapy. And Laura and I will be spending more time together than we have in a long, long time. Happy times are coming.

Anxious to go home, I find it impossible to sleep. It's three AM, and I decide to take a stroll down Tokyo's Shinjuku entertainment district to have a final taste of the hustle and bustle of this great city.

Today is the eleventh of the eleventh month, and this is celebrated throughout Asia as Bachelors' Day. The digit one resembles a stick, symbolizing someone who is alone; 11/11 is considered to be a lucky day for singles.

On Alibaba, Asia's answer to Amazon, countless bachelors today have bought more than two hundred million anti-Valentine's gifts at this year's Single's Shopping Festival. Funnily enough, many single people find each other on this special day and are henceforth no longer single. Even at this late hour, the streets are filled with happy couples, determined to paint the town red tonight. I feel energized just by watching this late-night public display of fun, but I can sense it is fueled by booze and a certain type of human despair.

The Japanese are known for their "work hard, play hard" attitude. They even have a dedicated word, *karoshi*, for death by overwork. Not just the strenuous office hours, but also the *nomikai* or after-hours drinking parties installed by management to build better connections between coworkers are known causes of sudden mortality through heart attacks.

On the few occasions this past month when I found myself on the very last train leaving Tokyo center at night, it was full of near-comatose drunken salarymen. Not a pretty sight. Especially here, in Shinjuku's red-light district of Kabukicho, the stress accumulated during a horribly long workday at one of the soul-consuming Japanese corporate behemoths like Sony or Toyota finds an escape in adult entertainment of a type that we Westerners find bizarre yet intriguing.

I walk past all-night karaoke bars, decadent cross-dressing cabarets, hot strip clubs, erotic massage parlors, and, of course, the infamous soap lands, which are in reality typical Tokyo brothels, disguised as ritualistic bathhouses.

The men that frequent the Shinjuku soap lands pretend to go there to get a spa treatment, but everybody knows what really takes place and how the soap gets applied. The unavoidable probing for feedback on a foreigner's first soap land experience the morning after the event never fails to trigger giggles from the Japanese office ladies and knowing smiles from the Tokyo hosts who'd arranged the escapade for their unsuspecting visitor.

The many places of vice that I walk past are populated with Tokyo salarymen, but I also see Western men eager to get a taste of the excitement. Abundant drinking takes away all of their inhibitions, and, even if they might regret their promiscuity the day after, for now, they are enjoying the female company. And it is a well-known fact that Japanese ladies love tall white foreigners as companions for the evening, especially because Westerners are more likely to openly pursue women, compared to the more passive, introvert Japanese men.

I am walking through the busy streets, and all the while these thoughts are running through my mind. Although it's tempting, I still know better than to enter one of the Shinjuku bars. The new and improved me absolutely wants to keep it clean. I am here only to observe and enjoy the unique ambience. I stroll up Love Hotel Hill or Dogenzaka, which is sprinkled with miniscule, rent-by-the-hour lodgings with bizarre decors. I look at the screen displays near the doors of the love hotels, and I see some even offer extras like costume rental to play out any desired fantasy. I marvel at so much kitsch concentrated in one place.

As I walk on, I soon find myself in Golden Gai, a time-warped collection of two hundred tiny theme bars tucked away in six alleyways in old Tokyo, which form the core of the hard-drinking party scene. Each bar can barely fit ten people and has its own particular vibe and outlandish decor. The buildings are ramshackle and dwarfed by high-rise developments all around, but this place has something magical. I peek my head in one of the bars and see that it is crammed with five couples listening to a girl with a violet hairdo playing 1980s vinyl records. Weird does not even begin to describe it.

This place attracts me, simply because it is a no-go zone for someone in recovery, someone like me. It feels great to bite the forbidden apple for once. I keep telling myself that as long as I stay dry, there is no problem with being here. In a couple of hours, I will go to the airport, and that will be that.

But on some deeper level, I can't help but wonder what brought me here on my last night in Japan. My going off the beaten path tonight does somehow feel intentional. As if I want to prove that I'm back amongst the living and nothing is off limits anymore, not even this. I'm hardened, and I can handle myself in any situation.

But can I?

I know I have to be cautious since my senses are already in overload, just by being exposed to the sheer restlessness of these streets. The annoying bell sounds originating from the many vertical pinball machines in the *pachinko* arcades trigger my nerve endings. The loud, drunken laughter, the Karaoke singing, and the constant rapid chatter in Japanese coming from every bar are putting me on edge.

Despite the frantic nature of the surroundings though, I find myself enjoying the dizzying freedom that comes from wandering all alone in a completely alien city, deep into the night. I take a deep breath of night air and look up at the sky. I cannot see the stars because the neon lights are blinding my night vision.

I feel hungry, so I walk into a steaming ramen shop and order a hot bowl of *kakesoba*, the delicious Japanese lobster noodle soup. The uncut ocean flavor of the seafood ramen at this time of night somehow strikes me as fully congruent with the strange and unfamiliar settings I find myself in. I cannot help but smile while eating my soup and watching the passersby. It feels good to be completely anonymous and yet part of the scenery.

When I leave the ramen shop, I wonder what to do next at this ungodly hour. I definitely do not feel sleepy, and I decide to pull an all-nighter. I can sleep on the plane home. I feel a piece of paper in the pocket of my suit. An expat colleague has given me the address of a fabulous skyline bar at the top floor of the Tokyo Park Hyatt where Coppola's indie movie *Lost in Translation* was filmed.

I start to walk slowly in that direction until I find myself standing in front of the Hyatt. I hesitate to go in. Why am I going to a bar? Because the view is said to be fantastic, of course. And I just love that movie. I think I've seen it five times because it captures expat life in a foreign metropolis to perfection. After some further deliberation, I cross the imposing but empty lobby and take the elevator up to the fifty-second floor, straight into the glorious bar where Bill Murray first saw Scarlett Johansson sitting on her own, feeling bored while her husband was out working.

I have a soft spot for Scarlett, and I imagine myself in the iconic movie scene right when Bill offers her a Suntory single-malt Japanese whisky—"For relaxing times, make it Suntory time"—and she teasingly orders a vodka and tonic instead, with that flair of feminine defiance that would become her signature expression.

I look around and to my surprise, the bar has a glitzy Gatsby theme going on, with the women dressed in the iconic '20s flapper style with bobbed hair and dazzling short sequin shift dresses. I am immediately attracted by the atmosphere of the place, and, as nobody seems to stop me, I walk up to the bar.

An elegant blond in a flamboyant red Roaring Twenties dress is singing Lana Del Rey's "Young and Beautiful," accompanying herself on a white Baby

Steinway. While she's an absolute stunner and a great singer, nobody pays any attention to her. Nobody but me, that is. In fact, I cannot keep my eyes off her. That risqué red dress has me in a spell. After a couple of minutes, I do start to feel like a voyeur, and, with some effort, I manage to pull my gaze away from her.

I cannot help but notice that the guests are sipping from Vintage 1920 Prohibition Cocktails like Highballs and Old Fashions, Daiquiris, and Side Cars. The stylish drinks look cold and enticing and serve as the perfect catalysts to stir up the intended wild and carefree 1920s ambience.

It's an oddly international crowd. I hear male voices talking Swedish, English, and German, while the female sounds are distinctly Russian, Balkan, and Japanese.

The girls are wearing stiletto heels under their sleeveless, short-skirted flapper dresses with deep open backs. They have feathers in their hair, and some are wearing diamond tiaras and long pearl necklaces. Most are smoking long cigarettes, although smoking is strictly prohibited here. Nobody seems to care. Most of the men are wearing 1920s tuxedos, while some others are in striped suits and flashy neckties, sporting Vintage Rolex Oyster and Vacheron Constantin watches.

One impressive-looking man with silver hair and a heavy Australian accent is apparently the host for the evening. He is dressed in all white, just like the Great Gatsby himself. Our host is walking around with a cigar in his mouth, a smile on his face, and a Martini in both hands.

The woman he's with has clearly gone to great lengths to be a perfect Daisy Buchanan, Jay Gatsby's dream girl. She's wearing a bejeweled dress in taupe, fingerless lace gloves, an Art Deco headband, and a pastel blue fur collar. She's laughing and spills her drink while slowly dancing to the music, clearly in a state well beyond tipsy.

I find myself alarmingly aroused by all of this. Somehow it feels like coming home. As I stand there watching this upper-scale crowd, I cannot believe that I actually party-crashed a glamorous jet-set extravaganza in a Tokyo skyline bar at four in the morning and nobody stopped me. Maybe because of the late hour, they do not care anymore who joins. Or maybe I just belong here. Thank God I'm wearing a black Tom Ford suit.

The contrast of this elegant and classy venue with the seediness in the streets below could not be bigger. And yet, the whole sequence of events of this Tokyo night has a kind of surreal logic to it, as if I'm in a lucid dream where all of this makes perfect sense. I look through the bar's high windows at Tokyo's skyline. It is truly formidable, and I feel drunk with excitement.

The bartender has noticed me and gestures me to take a seat. Before I can ask him whether this really is the *Lost in Translation* cocktail lounge, he nods affirmatively and points to a specific bar stool. I am obviously not the first guest to have recognized the bar from the classic movie.

When I ask "He or she?" he answers with a tired smile, "She," while pointing to the exact bar stool that Scarlett occupied in the iconic scene.

I take that seat and order a Kirin Ice beer with a very exact 0.0% alcohol. I have been sober for eighteen long months now, and I'm here on the premise that I'm sufficiently ruggedized to be trusted alone in a late-night Tokyo bar. I realize I did not discuss this upfront with Dr. Lavorter, and something tells me that I should have. But who am I fooling? Deep down, I can feel the familiar sting in a place like this. Like an old love lost but not forgotten, it still eats at my core. It cannot be a coincidence that I go back to watering holes like this. I'm deliberately seeking the thrill that comes with this sort of place.

Well, I might as well try to enjoy it while I'm here.

Three pretty Japanese girls, all in black-and-white Tuxedo dresses with little black bow ties, are entertaining five German businessmen at the far end of the bar, away from the party. I wonder whether these girls are hired extras. They seem too beautiful to be true. They look like identical triplets, in their pristine dresses and impeccable makeup. They even have the same height and near-perfect proportions. I cannot help but wonder at this arrangement.

On the surface, the men look like predators. They are alpha males, in town this week to close the deal. They're loud and over-confident. The girls seem too young and outnumbered. They display a look of over-the-top vulnerability, and my gut says this is all make-believe. It seems choreographed to perfection.

I watch as an eight-hundred-dollar jeroboam bottle of Roederer Cristal Champagne gets passed around in their small circle and keeps them going. After a couple of minutes, I realize that it's actually the girls who are in the lead here. The men are powerless and can only give way to their primal instincts in this age-old ritual of seduction. The girls are flirting shamelessly, as she-wolfs in their natural habitat. Female power is the dominating force here.

I know this little scene that plays out here all too well. It triggers an old ambiguity in me. I want to watch and look away at the same time. With both shame and fascination battling for my attention, I sense a familiar but uneasy duality. But why should I care anyway? This has nothing to do with me.

The bartender minds his own business, and I, too, turn away. But only reluctantly so.

My heart starts beating faster, like it is out of control. What I'd really want more than anything else is to step into this scene. I want to join the posse and sharpen my hunting skills. I want to give way to my inner predator. I want to drop the façade and follow my deeper drifts.

I want to drink and feel alive and connected.

I am now utterly confused, as I can feel an old fire within me gaining strength. I want a drink—there is no denying that simple fact. My eyes settle on a glass cabinet with expensive cigars on display. Each cigar is wrapped individually with an impressive label that reads "Caliber & Carat" in an elegant font.

My mind connects dots which are not there. Caliber as in lethal weapon, and carat as in flawless diamond. Or carat as in flawless girl and caliber as in character strength?

I feel a flash of anger coming up suddenly. What type of man would mess around with girls this young, very late on a weeknight? But then I wonder whether that man could be me under different, less-sober circumstances. Anger quickly turns into guilt. Am I really considering a drink after eighteen months of hard work at sobriety? And would I really chase those young women then, fueled by liquid courage?

My gaze drifts back to the three Japanese girls at the far end of the bar, and I see, to my surprise, that one of them is also watching me. She gives me a seductive look while she pulls one of the German men closer by his tie and kisses him on the mouth without hesitation. Then she teasingly looks over her shoulder back at me, and her black eyes dare me: "You want a taste of this?"

I suddenly feel freaked out, as if any minute now, I will be exposed as an imposter. I am totally out of place here. Surely, the entry ticket to this bar must be a real drink, an adult drink! And that is the one thing I cannot have. Whoever has let me in here made a serious mistake. I feel like a total miscast, a fraud.

With thoughts spiraling down into a familiar, destructive pattern, I quickly pay for the fake beer, which I did not touch. The barman really does not care and gladly accepts my tip.

It occurs to me I am still a dry drunk, full of resentment and anger.

I've come so close, so very, very close, to giving in. The remaining barrier between me and a drink is only wafer-thin. My defenses are down; I'm completely exposed. It's clear that this place eats at my resolve and that I need to leave.

Now.

I put on my raincoat, and I leave in a hurry. The higher-pitched broken English of the girls follows me into the corridor and seems to resonate all the way down the elevator ride.

The lift construction in glass is mounted against the front of the building, and, as I descend the fifty-two levels, I look outside at Shinjuku's nightlife, coming up ever closer. Seeing the party crowd on the streets no longer lifts my spirits. Quite the opposite. It looks like a real threat.

Once outside, I walk briskly in the general direction of my own hotel, feeling deeply sorry for myself. And

God knows that feeling sorry is not a good state to be in, not if I want to make it to the morning without a drink.

It starts to rain. First only a drizzle, but soon it's really pouring down on me. I almost cannot see through my glasses, and I bump into some drunken guy, who angrily pushes me away while shouting something in Japanese. The people around us stop to watch as if they would welcome a fight.

The rain is soaking me through and through, but I do not mind. This downpour feels utterly appropriate, like a ritualistic cleansing. Like I'm offered a chance to wash the dirt off me.

Once back in my room, I am far too agitated to go to bed. I simply watch the stock ticker on CNN while I gather my thoughts and try to come to some conclusion.

What to make of this? I walked out of an extremely tricky situation, this time. But what about next time? I almost lost it tonight. Within the hypermagnetic field of that cocktail bar, my moral compass was spinning around uncontrollably. And the feeling of disorientation was not only about the drinking—there was something greater at stake here. "Honor" is the word that comes to mind.

But wait just a minute here. After all is said and done, it seems my compass may still be pointing to the North. After all, I did not give in. I did not drink, and I definitely did not hit on the girls. It's not because I was tempted that I should feel bad now.

Yet the old, familiar question remains. In the final analysis, will I drink again? I've just had a taste of temptation like never before. Can it be that the urge will be even stronger the next time and the time after that? Until it is just humanly impossible for me to resist?

I take deep breaths and slowly but surely find myself back on solid ground.

I made it back alive from behind enemy lines. Back in the DMZ of my room, I now feel better about this whole thing. I walk to the window of my hotel suite, and I see the sun rise on Tokyo's grand Shinto shrine, dedicated to Emperor Meiji and his empress Shoken, who opened up Japan to the West. The shrine is located in an evergreen forest, cleverly hidden within the densely built-up city.

Yes, temptation was a clear and present danger tonight, and yet it did not tip me over. I came precariously close to giving in, and that realization hurts but feels good at the same time.

Deep down I know that I am and will always be like the moth circling the flame, unable to stay away from the brightest of lights.

CHAPTER 26

EPILOGUE

BY CATHERINE LAVORTER

At the time I write these final words, Peter has been sober for a good four years. Although he came close on a couple of occasions, he never relapsed. And I dare to say that he will not drink in the future. He made a safe ascent to the apex of sobriety and planted his flag at the summit. That is something that nobody can ever take away from him.

What he learned the hard way during therapy was that once alcohol, his drug of choice, was gone, he quickly found something else to obsess about. In his case, he went on a relentless quest to find the meaning of a sober life.

I believe that during Peter's treatment, we succeeded in doing away with the many misconceptions that ruled his thinking (remember the six bullets) and in parallel, Peter himself learned to appreciate and use his intuition, his sixth sense, to balance out his typical black-and-white logic.

Peter's and Laura's marriage survived the rough times of rehab and recovery, and their sabbatical in India with the volunteering work allowed them to learn to appreciate and love each other in new ways, without the need to constantly look back and yearn for the good old times, before the drinking. Wolf and Winter, their children, have each gone their own way but with a renewed sense of respect for their father ever since they realized he was making good on his promise to abstain.

After the sabbatical, Peter rejoined his previous company and is now again traveling the world. He started a blog on which he shares his travel impressions and philosophical broodings with a growing contingent of followers.

Adaline Vikander successfully completed her Ph.D and now works as a Junior Partner in my practice. She has her own set of patients and lets me sit in at times when I myself am looking for inspiration, especially when she is using mindfulness and Buddhist meditation to complement traditional therapy. She told me she's seriously thinking of writing a book of her own.

I hope that the reader sees this story as one of hope. Recovery statistics in general paint a dismal picture and suggest that three out of four addicts relapse in the first year of sobriety, but Peter's story shows that it can be done. He has built a life away from addiction and is no longer in a daily battle to remain sober. He has learned to some extent how to let go and to come home to himself.

If you yourself are to embark on this sobering ascent, make sure you do not go it alone. Prepare your journey well, make sure you take sufficient time to acclimatize to the new heights, and most of all, get a guide to go with you to the mountaintop. Your chances of reaching it will be so much higher.

Allow me to end with a quote by another famous mountaineer, Michael Kennedy: "Big alpine routes aren't exactly safe . . . You need to have your feelers out, and you need to be willing to back off if things aren't quite right. At the same time, you have to push through your doubts and fears. Only then will you safely reach the summit."

ACKNOWLEDGMENTS

To my wife Natja: Because I owe it all to you, darling. Love you to the moon and back.

To my daughter Monika and my son Alexander: I know both of you are strong and you will make it in life. Trust yourselves and each other.

I am grateful to my late mother, Paula, and my late father, Maurice, who have provided me with moral and emotional support in my life. I am also thankful to my brother Paul and my sister Annelies, who have supported me on the road to recovery.

A very special thanks goes out to my therapist Myriam Bruyninckx for the many hours of listening and endless discussions, and to my former boss Dirk Van den Berghen for his patience and support.

Big thanks to my writing coach Stuart Horwitz for believing this work could be important in order to help others.

With a special mention to my friends throughout Asia. What a marvelous place to work!

AUTHOR BIO

*P*hilip Muls is a senior business executive in a global
corporation, who has been traveling on the job through
Asia for the last twenty-plus years. He holds an MBA from
Leuven University and has been granted various sales and
management awards in the software industry.

After quitting alcohol in his mid-forties, Philip started to
research and experiment with a variety of recovery treatments
on the level of mind and body and also on the level of his
deeper self.

This book blends his amazing travel stories with an
authentic account of how alcohol affects the brain and how
recovery from addiction can be like navigating a minefield
of existential fears and obsolete beliefs.

When he is not off traveling in China or India, Philip
lives with his wife Natja and his two children Monika and
Alexander in Grimbergen, Belgium.

Made in the USA
San Bernardino, CA
30 July 2018